2008

Happy Christ

Tales from a Suitcase

Tales from a Suitcase

Will Davies &
Andrea Dal Bosco

Lothian
BOOKS

Thomas C. Lothian Pty Ltd
132 Albert Road, South Melbourne, Victoria 3205

First published 2001
Reprinted 2003

National Library of Australia
Cataloguing-in-Publication data:

Tales from a suitcase.

ISBN 0 7344 0237 6.

1. Immigrants – Australia – Biography. 2. Immigrants – Australia – Anecdotes. 3. Australia – Emigration and immigration – Biography. I. Davis, Will. II. Dal Bosco, Andrea.

305.90691

Design and typesetting by Sandra Nobes
Front cover colourisation by Sam Young
Printed in Australia by Griffin Press

Contents

Preface

Imagine this.

You have just survived the war, in which you lost everything. Many members of your family were killed, some died in camps; others, you just don't know about. Many of your neighbours have disappeared. Your house is now little more than a pile of rubble. All you own is what's on your back, but all the same you are thankful to be alive after three very long years in a displaced persons camp where your constant companions were sickness and the cold.

Your homeland has gone, taken over by the communists and absorbed into one of the new socialist countries behind the 'Iron Curtain'. You are homeless, stateless and virtually destitute.

You weigh your options. At the point where everything seems so meaningless and hopeless you hear of a faraway land, unscathed by war, that is looking for workers. A place where you can start a new life. A place called Australia.

Australia? Where is it? What is it? Someone tells you it's near the South Pole; someone else tells you that it's where kangaroos come from. You eventually discover that it is at the bottom of the world, remote, hot and with the seasons around the wrong way.

But the possibility of a new life, another chance, in a land where there is work and peace, is too great an opportunity to let go. The war is barely over and already there is talk of another war, the Cold War. So, with no idea what it will mean and what it will be like, you decide to go — the further away, the better. The queues are shorter for Australia — certainly shorter than for America and Canada — and it is warmer there, they say: a nice change from the bitter cold of northern Europe. You apply.

You fit the criteria: you're young and healthy, free of tuberculosis and educated; you are neither a communist nor a criminal and you already have a few words of English. They tell you you're welcome, but there is a catch: if you want to migrate, you must agree to sign a contract to work at the direction of the government for two years. You will be designated a 'labourer' and your wife a 'domestic'. If you break your contract or return to your homeland before your time is up, you will owe the government for your passage. This is serious but what have you got to lose?

You sign up and start to pack. The weight limit is strict: fifty kilograms per person and that is all. What do you take? What are the most important fifty kilograms of your life? What will you need in this new land? Will the weather be hot or cold when you arrive? How do the people dress? And anyway, how will you fit all you need into those small suitcases? The time for such decisions begins to run out.

The day arrives. You stand in one of the lines on the wharf with many just like you. All of you are wondering what lies ahead, on the sea voyage and in a new life, far from family and friends. You don't know when or whether you'll return. In the silent throng you all look the same: strangely pathetic, apprehensive, clutching bulging suitcases of faded leather, carpetbags and bundles of tightly wrapped bed linen.

Once aboard, you find yourself deep in the bowels of the ship without air or natural light, in a cabin that is small and dank — always dark, always grim . . . and, though shared with others, somehow lonely.

The voyage seems endless. The smell of vomit and engine fumes are never far away and the metal sides of your narrow bunk quiver with the distant thump of the engines. The long propeller shaft, you realise, must somehow pass close by; the air has a static buzz that makes your hair frizz and your skin crawl. You never get comfortable, you never sleep.

Over the days, the weeks, the dull grey sea slowly changes to a deep aqua and then a cobalt blue. You have tired of the curling wake and the long line of churn behind the ship and the diving seabirds. As the seas warm, the rare sight of tropical flying fish comes as a fresh visual escape.

Then the ports start to go by and the ship docks. All vibration momentarily stops, as does the stench of shipboard life. From the grubby port, another unknown stench: putrid water, salt and slime. Then away. Where to next?

Another port. Far below, boys dive for coins that spin endlessly from high decks above. Maybe the rich have a coin to tempt these youngsters. You have nothing. Pedlars fight for space by the seaward stairs that descend to the waterline, selling exotic trinkets you have never seen before and cannot imagine a need for. You want to move on, you want to get to this place called Australia and get on with life — whatever that might be now.

The days take on a rhythm. There are things to do, now that you know where to find them. Movies on Australia are being shown — weird flickering images from faded film reels that chatter behind you, images of smiling faces, beaches, kangaroos (yes, you know what these are) and strange-looking houses. There are also English classes to go to, and talks about your new country. (Years later, you will reflect on how many now-familiar words were missing from these classes — words like 'wog' and 'reffo' and 'wop' and 'dago' and 'commie' . . .)

Fremantle. So *this* is Australia! The lay-over is short, but the country has an aroma you've never known before. The circling, screeching seagulls swoop and dive in warm air thick with the scent of eucalyptus. The people seem informal, even rude, but they know how to relax and they seem proud.

Now you are being processed as an immigrant. Officials swarm about the boat, speaking in a way that neither you nor your fellow passengers understand. There is a desperate need for more translators. Tempers fray and apprehension and confusion rise. Facing arrival, you realise how comfortable you have grown with your little cabin on your smelly little ship.

The southern sea from Perth to Melbourne is like dark ink and constantly rough. It heaves and swells, again making all on board sick and wishing for landfall. The immigration officers continue to ask questions. You have many questions of your own, but your language skills, although improved, do not allow you the confidence to speak.

The ship slides into that quiet, open bay: Port Phillip. The sea is grey again, but calm. Gulls circle and scream, much as they did in Perth, uttering a universal language — perhaps a welcome.

From Station Pier, ramshackle and uninviting, inquisitive faces stare up: the dark, tanned faces of Australians or the olive-skinned complexion of southern Europeans, you know not which. Eventually the cacophony of noise from the chatter of voices and the constant whirr of the engines gives way to silence and you can hear again.

Then that first footstep ashore. You feel wobbly and ill-at-ease on the hard asphalt of the wharf. Your sea legs are of no use here; they let you down. Other folk stumble and fall. Off to your left, there is a call for workers — strong, unskilled men — to work in a brick pit somewhere. There are no takers, but it is good to know work is readily available.

You and your possessions — both increasingly inadequate — are directed towards a row of ageing buses at the end of the wharf. It has been some time since breakfast and you are hungry — but not so hungry as those who missed the last ship meal, clinging to the rail, searching for answers through the dawn haze smudging the line of the shore. Your line shuffles forward, one small pace at a time, until you are on a bus. Crammed in, you all stare through the misty windows to the street outside. The air thickens with acrid cigarette smoke and the pungent odour of sweat. Seated above the rear wheel, you feel the broken surface of the road as you lurch and bump over the silver tramlines that score the city streets.

Then there is the sight of a train: a large, belching steam engine and a line of dirty maroon carriages waiting for you. Trains still have dark overtones for many and there is a certain reluctance and silent concern about boarding for an unknown destination.

Given no choice, you steam out through the suburbs. First, the tiny slum suburbs of inner Melbourne with their peeling paint, rusting ironwork and tin roofs. Further out, enclosed backyards with small outbuildings — could these possibly be toilets? — arranged along the fence lines like silent sentries. The city looks drab, but there is no sign of the war damage of your homeland.

A place called Albury and another bus. Finally you reach a holding camp, Bonegilla. This is where you will wait, for God knows how long. Originally built for the army, it is devoid of comforts and its functional layout belies its unhappiness. You are issued with a hut and told to remember the number, as they all look the same. The amenities are Spartan yet adequate. Mealtime takes care of your hunger, even if the food is unlike anything you have ever tasted before. Soft, white bread, boiled vegetables and endless mountains of mutton. The smell of mutton fat seems to cling to your hair and lips — it won't go away. Some heave and vomit up their food.

You ask about work and when you might start. You know they can send you anywhere to do anything and you wonder about your fate. Your qualifications as an engineer will be ignored and you wish you had a trade — were a carpenter or a stonemason — as they need these skills. Your wife is a teacher and she has asked about the local school, but there is little chance. They need a woman in the hospital laundry, she is told. At least this is close to the camp. You are selected to go east to the new Snowy Mountains Scheme. The mountains, the vastness of the scheme and the offers of plenty of shifts and lucrative pay sound attractive. You go.

But it is hell. Home, in Guthega, is a tent in mid-winter, with the snow two metres deep. You work in a wet, dank tunnel deep underground where screaming drill bits and explosives split the air. Didn't they say Australia had a warm and comfortable climate?

You wonder why you came, but then you remember: you are free here, you are no longer hungry, you live a strong and healthy life among fellow migrants and friendly Australians. Though you are new to this place, you already feel a certain attraction as you build the country — actually build it and change it and make your mark.

And in two years you will be free of the government contract, free to build your own life, your own home, your own family. At last you feel that a future is possible and that this future is truly in your hands.

You are proud to be a 'new Australian'.

WD & ADB

Acknowledgements

This book comes from the research and filming undertaken in the production of the SBS Independent program, *Tales from a Suitcase*, series two. This is a follow-up to the first '*Tales*' series, which first went to air in late 1996, to popular acclaim and good ratings, and has since been repeated a number of times.

Our thanks in producing the series go first to SBS Independent, especially Courtney Gibson and Sashka Koloff, to Rod Webb for his continuing support and to Andy Lloyd James who originally supported the idea of a continuing migrant oral history series. To Henry Tefay at the Pacific Film and Television Commission in financially supporting the series and the two Queensland directors who contributed two episodes each.

To the production team: Simone Uhlhorn, the production manager and researcher, Roman Baska the director of photography, Bernard Ashby the Series Editor, John Russell our accountant and the four directors, Peter Hegedus, Debra Beattie, David Vadiveloo and Veronica Iacono who each researched and directed two episodes.

To Brian Cook from Lothian Books for chasing us up and to Sally Moss for following through.

To the Department of Immigration and Multicultural Affairs who gave us permission to reproduce their photographs, both as the opening title sequence in the series and as images in this book, and to the Minister, Philip Ruddock, for his enthusiastic endorsement of this project.

But our greatest thanks and praise go to the wonderful people who make up the subjects in our series, who kindly allowed us into their lives and who freely gave of their time to support this series. To them our sincere thanks, not only for this contribution, but also for their long and valued contribution to Australia. They, like hundreds of thousands of 'new Australians', have come and made a new home and have contributed so much to this nation. We hope their contribution, this television series and perhaps this book at least go some way towards bridging the gap between Anglo–Australian and migrant peoples, in order to help us all understand the immigrant experience a little better.

'Born Again'

The tale of Jutta Malnic

The first time, I was born in Berlin. At the time my father was Head of the Trade Department at the Foreign Office. My mother was born in Australia. My father held that, in her approach to life, she always remained 'a wild colonial girl' and was therefore a handful to him as a diplomat's wife. But he managed to put her independence aptly and splendidly to work for the purpose of his jobs. (There are many anecdotes to support this.)

The childhood stories that my mother told me were always about her Australian holidays in the bush. Most often these were at Burradoo [near Bowral, south of Sydney], in another of those houses with 'frowning inquisitive roofs' (looking into bedrooms) over the verandah. And I loved to live again and again through the excitement of my great-grandmother, driving the children in a horse and buggy through bushfires; or to hear of them lobster fishing at Eaglehawk Neck; or to imagine playing hopscotch on the wondrous tessellated pavement on the coast of Tasmania. Sunny New South Wales always sounded like heaven on earth.

From Berlin my father was transferred to Zurich as Consul-General. I went to school in Switzerland for four years and this actually became a very, very wonderful and memorable period of my life. In our free time we were always getting around within a small group of children — walking in the forest, flying kites, bob-sleighing and skiing in winter.

I believe that from 1933, the time Hitler came to power, there were problems for my father. Old-school diplomats did not bend like saplings to the new winds of the Third Reich.

Thirty-two times the house was on fire.
We became very good firefighters, mother and I.

Towards the end of 1934 my father died in Switzerland. We moved back to Berlin. The whole of my teenager years and schooling are more or less hazy.

I remember the first big bombing raid and my mother saying we'd better be up on the roof so we could see any fires and put them out straight away. Well, I was so scared that I still can't find words to describe it. Mother didn't have any fear. I don't know why. But this was the first and last time that we were lying up there, under the roof, with sharp hot things coming through the tiles over our heads. Let it burn, I said. So from then on we sheltered in the cellar and waited till it was all over. Only then did we go and put out the fires. Thirty-two times the house was on fire. We became very good firefighters, mother and I. It was quite a turn-on!

After we had extinguished the fires in our own house, we would go for a walk to see if other people needed help to put their fires out. Long after the war, someone told me that this joy at watching things burning causes a kind of sexual arousal. I can believe that. All those fires, the sight of those burning houses, they were probably the reason for a sexual awakening in me, too. You know, that joyous feeling when a fire is lit in your heart!

Every time we survived a bombing raid, it was like being born again, a birthday! Mother had endless little bottles of champagne; so every time we survived an air raid, we would share a little bottle of champagne and celebrate another birthday!

During the war, life was just bombing — literally day-by-day bombing — and not knowing whether you'd live on. There were no young men around to fall in love with. Or, if you did give someone a second glance, he would unfailingly go off to war and get killed or maimed. To me, flirting became equal to putting a jinx on a guy. The only stable beau in my life then was this beautiful statue of Alexander von Humboldt that I walked past every day on my way to university — the Alexander v Humboldt University Unter den Linden in Berlin.

Alexander von Humboldt was like the German equivalent of Charles Darwin. I read a bit about his work and discovered that he researched and explored in South America. I just liked the guy. And it was from that time that my idea of wanting to go into the South Pacific began to grow.

During the years after World War II, I just urged to get out of Berlin. I had lived in that city and breathed the dying dust of the war's unceasing implosions; I worked that city as a photojournalist. It was *my* city. But it stank. It was putrid. Berlin was rotten. There was every vice known to mankind thrown into the open. And there were the memories of the war, of so much fear, and of the Open City, street-by-street fighting in the last days of the war. Of burying people who died in the streets, between buildings. We buried quite a few bodies in the last days of the war and straight after. Dead bodies have to be put under the earth. They smell. Berlin felt like you were walking on an eternal putrid graveyard.

I wanted to get out and said to mother, 'Let's all go back to Australia.'

Mother did not want to go back to her birthplace. All her friends were interesting people from her diplomatic life. They lived all over Europe. And when she agreed to go back to Australia for her children's sake, she insisted on taking her furniture and arranged for everything to be flown out of Berlin. When it became known that Mother had chartered an aeroplane, half of Berlin (figuratively speaking) waited and looked up in the sky so that they wouldn't miss Mrs Windel's aeroplane. Unfortunately, that special flight was scheduled at the onset of the Berlin blockade. The Russians cancelled all individual planes. But mother got her furniture crates taken out on the empty return flights of the allied airlift into Berlin.

My sister Beate had been evacuated from the bombing in Berlin. She had spent her high school years with an aunt in Erfurt, in the middle of Germany. My brother Rudi was still at a boarding school in Switzerland. We wanted to get together again as a family, and get out. So we started the process of getting permits to go to Australia.

Mother was a British subject so she still held a British passport. But she also had a German passport because she was married to a German diplomat. In those days it was 'once a Briton always a Briton' but it still took two and a half years to get out of Germany, because the Australian Military Mission worked ever so slowly. In the end we paid for our trip ourselves and came out under our own steam on a private ship from Sweden.

We left Berlin in 1948 at the beginning of June. In Gothenburg, we joined MV *Parramatta*, a Swedish freighter. The journey to Melbourne took six and a half weeks, via the Cape of Good Hope, Cape Town, Durban, and Lorenzo Marques. The trip was wonderful. It was just like being children again, we siblings at last reunited.

So we left Germany behind. We died over it, we were born again and we truly 'started a new life in Australia', as the saying went at the time. I did not go back to Germany for another thirty-six years. And I never missed it.

When we first arrived in Melbourne, I remember that my godfather, uncle Ekke (Eckehardt Beinssen), had come from Sydney to welcome us and a couple of journalists had arrived at the ship. Uncle Ekke pushed them out of the cabin door and said, 'No, thank you. We don't want any press.'

They said, 'But you're going to get it anyway.'

On the ship, with this lasting postwar hunger psychosis, we had all gorged ourselves on fabulous Swedish food. My sister and I, we arrived as fat as maggots. The newspaper guys managed to get a picture of Beate and me, but without my mother. And the article that was printed started with: '. . . after years of hunger and starvation . . .' Our surname was Windel, but they wrote: '. . . after years of hunger and starvation Mrs. *Swindle* and her two lovely daughters arrive in Melbourne.'

Whenever it was cold in Berlin, Mother had always talked about sunny New South Wales. She would say, 'Now wait till we get to Australia. It'll be lovely and warm.' Well, Melbourne in August! I had never felt so cold, so thoroughly and permanently cold. And it was raining!

From Port Melbourne we were meant to catch a taxi to our hotel in the city. But there was only a Hansom Cab available — a horse-drawn cab. You climbed in from the back and you sat two-by-two opposite one another. The luggage was put on the roof. The cab was drawn by an old white horse.

We sort of chuffed and clop-clopped along the wet wharves and into the city like this. I remember, as we were crossing Collins Street, there on the tramlines the old horse slipped or stumbled and fell over and we all fell about inside the cab. The luggage came off the roof and we bundled out quickly. It was all a big hullabaloo! The police came and with the help of some bystanders they lifted the poor old horse back onto its feet.

We all packed back into the cab and after another block we arrived at the Oriental Hotel, I think (or was it the Occidental Hotel?), and we went in. We settled in the lounge and mother ordered two whiskies, one for my uncle and one for herself. The moment my uncle lifted the glass to his lips, a waiter came and snatched it out of his hand and said, 'Sir, you can't drink here. You are not a resident.' So mother and Ekke sneakily shared that one glass of whisky. This was not at all how I had imagined Australia.

The next day we caught the train to Sydney. Victoria had

a very smart train for the time, called the *Spirit of Progress*, with sleeper cars. We went off to bed in the evening, then, around midnight, the train stopped and we had to change to a New South Wales train because they had a different rail gauge. In New South Wales they still had the old trains, and their train was known as the *Spirit of Protest*. It was like something from the bushranger days — much polished brass and rattling — and we were shaken about. We laughed and laughed like kids on a roller coaster.

In the morning I looked out as the train passed through the bush. And for the first time I realised the great contrast with what we were used to in Europe, including rich lush greens. The Australian bush was all subtle olive green and blue–grey. But Mother was ecstatic.

'Look, the bush is in bloom!'

'Where?'

'There! Can't you see? There's wattle everywhere!'

I looked out of the window. There was a spot of yellow here and a spot of yellow there — that was all. I thought, 'Oh my God, what *is* this?'

We arrived at Sydney Central Railway Station. As I walked out, I was hit by the realisation that, by pushing the family to come back to Australia, I'd made the greatest

> In the morning I looked out as the train passed through the bush. For the first time I realised the great contrast with what we were used to in Europe, including rich lush greens. The Australian bush was all subtle olive green and blue-grey.

> On my first bite into a meat pie I was rapt. I thought this was the most perfect and compact form of serving a meal.

mistake ever. Not then, nor ever after, has Central Railway Square been architecturally impressive, but it was the big, dark red-brick (from memory) Marcus Clarke building that gave the death knell to my enthusiasm about coming to Australia. All I could think of was, How long will it take for all of us to go back to somewhere in Europe?

Uncle Ekke insisted that we see Sydney from the water, so we were going to cross the harbour to Manly by ferry. We got onto the ferry at Circular Quay. Ekke went to buy some lunch at the Quay. He came back with a paper bag full of meat pies. On my first bite into my pie I was rapt. I thought this was the most perfect and compact form of serving a meal. This was the first pie in my life, delicious and beautiful. I am still a great fan of meat pies.

Once the ferry went past the Heads, it occurred to me that anyone — even in a rowboat, if they wanted to — could leave through Sydney Heads and nobody would stop you. One could literally row to New Zealand, or wherever. This was freedom. Sydney Heads spelt freedom to me. It also occurred to me that Sydney was at the doorstep of the Pacific. This was the first time that I felt, well, maybe I can live here.

From Manly to the family house at Collaroy, we drove through Frenchs Forest. Suddenly mother shouted, 'Stop! Stop the car! Stop the car! The bush is in bloom!'

It was August then, and I looked around and thought we had stopped on a rubbish dump. It was all just sand, stones, a few twigs and nothing. We all clambered out of the car and mother said, 'Bush orchids! See if you can find more bush orchids, or some Melbourne boronia!'

I said, 'Where?'

Mother went down on her knees and we all went down on our knees. You really needed a magnifying glass to catch sight of and discern any blooms in this scrub. Now, I know how exquisite, ancient, wise and climate-adjusted Australian bush flora is, but when anyone said 'bloom' to me then, it meant 'BLOOM'! Not these minute bush flowers you could hardly see. Well, I thought, at least somebody is happy. Mother was happy.

This was a very important day in finding a foothold in Australia. I often think of people landing here and I don't mean necessarily the boat people or refugees, but people who come here with anticipation . . . what they have to go through and what it would take to make them feel that this is safe soil. Because, when you come here, you leave the soil that you were born to and that you identify with. They say that it's easier for a woman to adjust because if you have children in a country you establish a close relationship to that soil. The country becomes your country and you draw the essence from the soil, through you, into your baby.

The first place where we lived in Australia was Lilyfield — basically a working-class suburb in inner Sydney. It is very special in my memory, though our tiny terrace house was a bit hard to get used to when compared with our nice, huge (though bomb-damaged) apartment in Berlin.

This terrace house was on the corner of the street. When we arrived there, mother saw the gold-on-black, shiny sign at the door and shrieked, 'At last!'

The name of the house was 'The Embassy'. At the end of 1934, my father had just received his transfer as Ambassador to Belgrade when he died in Switzerland, so my parents never made it to the embassy. That's why my mother, with her indomitable sense of humour, had called out, 'At last!'

Inside, Ekke wanted us to listen to 'a most beautiful and extraordinary' piece of music on a record. 'You'll love this, Inge,' he said to his sister, our mother. We gathered in the tiny front room around this ancient record player on a high wooden stand and expectantly looked into the twisted His Master's Voice horn. Ekke lowered a gramophone head and sat the needle down onto a slow-turning seventy-eight record.

'You will hear the song of the Australian lyre bird,' he said — a bit tongue in cheek, I thought. The 'song' went something like this: '*SSShhh SShhh SSShhhh* (needle scratching on record), *krrrrrr-rrrr* (needle over crack in the record), *Ssshhhh*, beep beep, *SShhh SSShhhh krrrrrrr*, beep, *SShhh SSShhhh*, *krrrrrr*, beeeeeeeep.' All this repeated several times over the length of the recording.

We were in stitches of laughter, but mother was in seventh heaven to hear it. Included in the rent for The Embassy was one other record with the racy tune of 'The Whistler and his Dog'.

Well, that was that. And then, of course, the novelty of having daily deliveries like milk, bread and the newspaper put or thrown over the fence at the front door. Sometimes, from the sound, you thought something terrible had happened, but it was just the wail of the 'bottle ohhhhh!' or the 'vege-ohhhhh!' or the sharp noise announcing the 'Dry cleena! Dry cleena!' Everything came to the door or over the fence.

The neighbours were very nice — warm and so eager to help. They arrived instantly, offering assistance: the loan of a cup of sugar or anything we needed at any time of the day.

To our amazement, the lady next door never got out of hair curlers on weekdays. And she wore carpet slippers at all times. Not that we were in any way fashionable; more the opposite. But it was strange for us. And then on Saturdays, to our great surprise, we would see this lady stepping out with an elevated hair-do, her face miraculously transformed with lipstick and pancake make-up, accompanied by her husband. We hardly knew them as the same people, getting into their shiny black Cadillac, both dressed to the hilt. They were off to the races.

When I arrived in Australia, I was a trained photographer — and I came with some work experience. I had been to a photo school for two years and I had training as a photojournalist working for the picture press agency Mauritius, in Berlin.

In Australia, I very soon realised I couldn't work as a photojournalist, for various reasons. For a start, everything is a considerable distance from every other story source that would make a reportage worthwhile. In Europe, you could round up a story quickly, in hours or days. It also takes about two years before you really become savvy about what it means to be Australian and understand the Australian spirit. From what I've observed, I don't think any quick-visiting journalist from Middle Europe has ever been able to grasp any of the true Australian spirit.

At the end of 1948, I went into the office of the *Sunday Sun* in Elizabeth Street and saw the pictorial editor, Fred

It takes about two years before you really become savvy about what it means to be Australian and understand the Australian spirit.

Gardner. I asked if I could work there and he said no — they only had male photographers. They did in fact have a tremendous gaggle of well-known photographers, such as Ivan Ives, Steve Dunleavy and Bob Trenoweth.

The pictorial editor said, 'Nice talking to you Judy, but I say! Bye-bye for now. See you again.'

'Sure, I'll drop in again,' I said. And I did, for very snappy visits, about eight, ten times. One day, when I dropped in, something had happened. They were short of photographers and Fred Gardner said, 'Look, there's the Davis Cup tennis at White City. Can you go and get us some pictures of it?' He told me what I had to get — some shots of the tennis and some shots of the people — and all that with this enormous Speed Graphic camera, when I was used to working with a smaller Leica.

At White City, I didn't want to stay back with the other photographers, so I was wondering how to get close to the action without obscuring anyone's vision. I thought, Well the only way to get close without making a feature of myself is by getting down on my stomach with this big camera and crawling out there towards the players. I was close to the actual court and got some terrific shots of the tennis, but I was told later that the spectators who saw me would never forget this woman crawling like a Green Beret soldier in front of everyone.

After the Davis Cup, the *Sunday Sun* asked me to do some printing. I was the only woman in the room where we printed. The guys were used to being by themselves and talking among themselves in this common dark room.

I said to them, 'Look, go ahead and use whatever language you like. What I don't want to hear, I don't hear.'

But they were all very nice to me. One day — it was actually early in 1950 — I was in the darkroom when Steve Dunleavy came in from a job. Steve hoisted himself onto the rim of this large square basin containing our developing trays to cool his sore feet in the running water. We were all printing and then developing at this basin, and chatting, when someone brought up the question of where I had been during the war and where I had been during the bombing.

I told them I was in Berlin.

And what did I think about it?

I said, 'Look, first of all, you did all you could to save your own life.'

But I can still remember standing outside with my mother watching the planes coming towards us. Every time a plane was hit by German flak it looked like a moth burning in a candle flame. My mother would hold on to me and say: 'Another mother in Australia or in England will now be crying for her son.'

'I mean, we weren't standing there feeling triumphant,' I told them, 'cheering for victory over the enemy.'

Then it came out that two of these guys in the darkroom had been up there — they had been bombers. And we talked about it. I asked them how it felt up there and they got from me how it was on the ground. Maybe this talk was a kind of guilt exchange.

From then on I could do no wrong. I had this utter, utter protection from these guys. They showed me how they did things and I was one of their mob. I had a lovely time, until I was six and a half months pregnant with Nicola and told them that I was leaving.

They said, 'Why are you leaving?'

'I'm having a baby.'

'You're having a baby?'

'Can't you see?' I said.

And they came back with: 'Oh, we thought you were always that fat.'

In 1949 an Irishman called Desmond Mackey came to see me. He was going to have an exhibition of photographs at David Jones. He had big black and white prints of Dublin street life. They all needed retouching, extensive spotting and attention to problems on the negatives. I did that for him as a job.

After his exhibition finished, he called in to the office of Orient Line, hoping the shipping line would buy his photographs for their travel promotion. But he arrived in the advertising department at a moment when a disaster had struck. The boss had photographed, with a brand-new Leica, the arrival of the ship SS *Orcades* on her maiden voyage from England: *Orcades* entering through Sydney Heads and passing under the Sydney Harbour Bridge. The processing lab had pulled the 35-millimetre film through the enlarger still wet and scratched the emulsion from end to end. It was an absolute disaster. To his everlasting merit, this Irishman instantly forgot about selling his pictures and stepped into the situation with: 'Don't worry, I know the very person who can help you.'

That's how I was introduced to this shipping line and I sat there for weeks and weeks fixing, spotting and retouching their prints for them. While I was doing this, I dreamed about being a shipboard photographer. And in my mind I had worked out the logistics for it. Then one day I was called into the Orient Line office and offered the job of cruise photographer. I was on the first cruise ship out into the Pacific after the war. First port of call, Suva.

The first time we came to Fiji was absolutely wonderful. At the Beachcomber Hotel at Deuba, we joined with hula girls, singing and dancing and drinking all night. It was just like having stepped out of a Somerset Maugham story. The passengers just didn't want to leave, to go back to the ship. I don't think it ever happened again but that time SS *Orcades* departed at noon the following day, fourteen hours behind schedule! Two thousand Fijians stood on the wharf crying their eyes out when the ship finally left. That was really fabulous. Then, over the years, all this delight deteriorated into a replica of Fijian culture for show and the tourist dollar.

The cruise ship job entailed producing candid photographs of people — for example, of passengers shaking the captain's hand at a cocktail party — and then selling them. We printed between five hundred and seven hundred black and white postcard prints per day. I had three assistants: two working in the dark room and one on sales. We worked sixteen hours a day, so there wasn't too much time to enjoy ourselves, except that we could go on the tours for free.

From that time the South Pacific was my second home. I worked on seventy-two Sydney-to-Sydney cruises over a period of nearly twenty years. Cruises lasted four days, eight days or sixteen days and once a year there was the 36-day cherry blossom cruise to Japan.

During the periods at home I photographed weddings, children and family occasions. That, in a way, was a documentation of Australian society; by reference, it also documented the family cohesion of the white Australian establishment. There I started to sense that there was another Australian society and history that I wanted to understand.

I left the sea in 1969. By then my children had grown up and I was quite used to taking off to the warmer climates in the Pacific as soon as it got cold in Sydney. When the cruising stopped, I was unsure of what I was going to do from there on. The children said, 'You are always going overseas, Mum. Why don't you see your own country for once?' So I went on a tour to Arnhem Land and took some photographs of Aboriginal rock paintings.

I was more or less shooting from the hip, but when I brought the results home they became quite popular. I

I still fit in with people and places when I go to Germany, but at times it is like walking over my own grave.

suddenly was known to be a photographer of Aboriginal rock paintings. The archaeologist Elaine Godden invited me to co-author *Rock Paintings of Aboriginal Australia* as a photographer. That was the beginning of a very special sector in my life, another birthday.

In the years that followed I worked with the remarkable Aboriginal elder David Mowaljarlai on a book called *Yorro Yorro — everything standing up alive.* The term *Yorro Yorro* refers to the universal life force and the book is about Aboriginal culture concepts in the Kimberley region. These go right back to creation. I think it could well be the most complete history of the Aboriginal culture and it continues to sell well.

Looking back, I feel that I have given Australia a big part of myself. I have become an Australian. I have adopted Australia. As an individual I have adopted it to the last leaf on its trees.

I have never been tied to any particular group of people or any hub of prejudice and ideas. I still fit in with people and places when I go to Germany, but at times it is like walking over my own grave. There are still a few ghosts lurking there. In 1986 I went back for the first time. I went to look at my school. I visited our street, the building where we had lived, the house we saved so many times during the bombing years. But I did not belong there any more. It had all been mine in another life.

And I must admit, I must shamefully admit, that before the Berlin wall came down I could not join my friends in their rightful rage when they took me there. It wasn't my problem any more. I wasn't a Berliner at heart any longer. And yet, any problem concerning Berlin, any outrageous obstruction of freedom like the wall, *would* have eaten my heart out if we had not left.

From the very beginning of my professional life, my camera has opened doors to places and subjects I wanted to experience. The camera is the pencil I use to sketch a dimensional story. The camera in your hand is an invitation to look at life.

It's like this: the camera is a key, but somewhere deep within, the photographer has to find the door he or she wants to open. To me, in Australia as in the Pacific, photography has been the key to a kingdom. It made me, it rooted me in this country and made me understand the people and become part of them.

The camera is a key, but somewhere deep within,
the photographer has to find the door.

An Australian Greek Tragedy

The tale of Denis George

An angel once cried a tear that fell to earth and rolled into an oyster, creating the first pearl. Another myth tells of how moonbeams were once swallowed by an oyster and turned into the oldest known gem, which, for centuries, was considered the most valuable.

The pearl is the only gem that is ready to wear straight from nature. It requires no cutting or polishing, only the warmth of a woman's touch to ignite its inner glow.

It is believed that Cleopatra once bet Mark Anthony that she could devour the wealth of a whole country in just one mouthful and to win the wager she swallowed a pearl in a glass of wine.

To the ancient Greeks the pearl was the symbol of unsurpassed beauty and was associated with love and marriage.

To Western Australia the pearl is a valuable and successful industry, worth around $200 million each year.

To Denis George the pearl has been a key not only to his new country but also to a Pandora's box.

* * *

I was born in Constantinople, of Byzantine ancestry. There, my father was employed as a doctor with a German company that was building the Orient line from Constantinople to Baghdad. When the war between the Greeks and Turkey started in 1922, my father, my brother and I were caught in Konia, the ancient capital of the Ottoman Empire, and my father, being Greek, was immediately arrested by the Turks. He was due to be hung on a nearby hill when a position became vacant. I can remember the people hanging from trees and moving and shaking around. I remember that moment.

In Konia at that time, our house was one of the best in town. The Turks were led by Mustafa Kemal Pacha, the leader of the Turkish Resistance and the man who, as 'Kemal Ataturk' [literally father of all Turks], became the father of the Turkish nation today.

He occupied and commandeered our house as his headquarters and I remember the Turkish officers coming inside and throwing things this way and that, going into rooms and opening the doors. They pushed us all into a small room and my father was arrested and imprisoned in the stable with the horses. My job was to get him his meals.

One day, as I took my father his lunch, Kemal started to play a melody, some kind of classic one — I can't remember now. My father heard our piano being played and asked me, 'Who is playing the piano?' I told him I didn't know — just one of the Turks. So he told me to run quickly and bring him his violin. My father, when he was a student in Munich, had been fortunate to be able to buy one of the most beautiful violins — an Amati — so, naturally, he treasured it.

I took the violin down to my father in the stable and he started to play, to accompany Kemal's piano playing. When I went back up to the house, I heard a commotion. Kemal suddenly stopped playing the piano and started asking, 'What's that sound? What's that violin? Where is it coming from?' I knew of course it was my father playing and someone was sent down to bring him up.

I saw my father with the violin, holding it in his hand, walking inside, and thought he was in big trouble. Anyway, Kemal told him something and then they started to play. My father started to play violin and Kemal was playing the piano. Then, all of a sudden, my father goes 'tack-tack-tack' with the bow on the violin, saying that Kemal had made a mistake and to correct it. Next day, my father went from being a prisoner to being named a colonel of the Turkish Military Medical Services in the district.

Now about the violin. During World War II, as my sister was trying to escape a German blockade during the occupation, one of the German officers noticed that she had

The pieces [of my father's violin] somehow came back to my sister and I have them now in a little box. That little box for me symbolises not only the atrocities of humanity, but also the bones of my father.

that violin and recognised it as an Amati. He tried to grab it and as my sister resisted he grabbed it out of her hands, broke it on his knee, threw the pieces down and put my sister in a concentration camp. Anyway, many years later, the pieces somehow came back to my sister and I have them now in a little box. That little box for me symbolises not only the atrocities of humanity, but also the bones of my father.

In about 1926, after the war between the Turks and the Greeks had finished, there were a lot of refugee Greeks in Turkey. The Swiss Red Cross in Constantinople had organised the first transportation of people from Turkey and we found ourselves in Greece in a camp, where we would live for quite a few years. Life in the camp, as in any camp, was not the best but we made the most of it.

Later, my father was appointed director of a hospital outside Salonica and there I attended the village school next to the hospital. Gradually things improved for us. We built a little house and from then on I was able to continue my studies at the high school (or gymnasium). During that period, I joined an athletics group with the name of 'Hercules'. Now, this group later took part in the running of the Olympic flame from Greece to the 1936 Olympic Games in Berlin and I was one of the runners.

In 1938, I had to serve my National Service in the Greek Army and then I was demobilised and put in reserve until the war started in Europe in 1939. Initially, Greece was quiet and when the Germans came they stayed in the north. A few years earlier, Mussolini had occupied Albania, a little nation just to the north-west of Greece, because the Albanians could not resist them. Mussolini had a plan to establish a Mediterranean Empire, as at this point everything was going all right for him. I was called back into the army.

One night I got drunk and went home to sleep, but I had only slept for a few hours when my mother woke me up saying, 'Wake up, wake up — war.' The Italians were bombing us, so I ran out of the house. I went to join my unit and I was sent to the Albanian front.

* * *

When World War II began, Greece took a neutral stance. But this neutrality ended when Italy invaded in 1940. The Italians came in through Albania, which they had occupied eighteen months earlier. The outnumbered, but determined, Greek Army soon pushed the Italians back into Albania, forcing the Germans to come to the aid of their allies. By the middle of 1941 Greece was occupied by a brutal tripartite of Italian, German and Bulgarian forces.

In September 1941 the Greek Communist Party founded the National Liberation Front (EAM), which signalled the birth of one of the best underground resistance movements in all of Europe. The military arm of EAM was known as the National Popular Liberation Army (ELAS).

* * *

When I was fighting against the Italians in April 1941, Churchill sent a small expeditionary force to Albania to help us, but Hitler attacked with twenty Panzer divisions and so we found ourselves in the middle between two fires: the fire from the Germans behind and that from the Italians in front. The Italians now become very brave and, as we could not resist, we started retreating through the mountains to save our lives. Going towards Salonica, I could not get through the German lines, so I joined the Allies — the Australian 6th Division — who were also retreating.

When I was in Larisa, I was bombed and partly buried and someone from the 6th Division who saw my leg moving pulled me out of the wreckage and put me in a truck. From the bombing, I suffered amnesia so they took me a few miles out of Larisa and dropped me on the side of the road with a canteen of water and some dry biscuits and bully beef. That was the best they could do because they had their own problems and were being chased by Stuka dive bombers.

Somehow I recovered and started to make my way south towards Athens with everyone else. I joined the Australians again in an olive grove, where the Germans continued to bomb us. After a desperate stand at the famous Narrows of Thermopylea, close to Marathon, I tried to get to Athens by passing to Peloponnisos in a boat, but this was sunk by the Stukas in the middle of the Gulf of Corinthos and I had to swim to the shore.

Here, in a little village, I was recognised, amazingly, by someone who had a photo of me from his son, Delfino, who had been killed early in the action. The family looked after me well and a few days later I left and headed for Athens. However, on reaching the Canal of Corinthos, German paratroopers came down and occupied the strategic bridge in the narrows. I was again in a mess and so returned to my friend's family.

I spent a week recovering, then, together with six other soldiers, made plans to go to Crete, where the allies had retreated. On reaching the east coast of the Peloponnisos, we commandeered a small sailing boat, but we had great difficulties as nobody knew how to sail. Somehow we managed to reach Crete, in Maleme, just as German paratroopers landed, some in Greek uniform. I still had my gun, so I joined the fighting.

I was wounded again and lost consciousness. When I came to, I found myself in a German plane flying to a makeshift field hospital with other wounded Germans. Their casualties were extremely heavy and later I heard that Hitler was almost ready to stop his attack on Crete. In the hospital, I pretended to be dumb, an idiot that did not know anything — and if I could not speak, I could not answer. Finally, during an allied air raid, I managed to escape, went to Athens and disappeared amongst the other Greeks in the city.

When I escaped from the German hospital, I was still suffering amnesia from the bombing. I could remember everything that had happened after the bombing, but not who I was, where I came from or who were my relatives.

One day, a gentleman stood in front of me and said, 'Dino, Dino, Dino!'

I said, 'Sorry, sir. I don't know you.'

'I'm your brother-in-law,' he said.

I said, 'Sorry, sir. With all respect, I don't know you.'

He said, 'Come with me.'

And there at his home, under the care of my sister, who had been released from the camp, I started gradually to remember — but not all, because even today, after sixty years, I have a lot of blank periods that I cannot recollect.

A few weeks later, when I was walking down the street, a gentleman stopped me. He said that he had been my professor in high school in Salonica — and did I remember him. He asked me what I was doing and I said, 'Sir, we are slaves now. What can we do? We must fight.'

And the professor said, 'Look, I've just escaped from the

prison myself and with others I am organising a resistance. Would you like to join it?'

I said, 'By all means.'

I told him where I lived and he said a man would come to tell me the code signal and I should follow him and do what he says. Soon after, a man came, gave me the code name and said, 'Welcome, come with me.' I went with him, this way and that, double-crossing the streets, until finally we ended up somewhere in an apartment where about twenty old fellows, thin like matchsticks, were sitting on the floor as there were not enough chairs.

They said, 'Welcome. We have a good report of you — you've been a soldier?'

'Yes, sir.'

'Can you fight?'

'Yes, sir.'

'You want to fight?'

'Yes, sir.'

'Well, you're the man we're looking for.'

So they put in front of me a map of Athens divided into seven sections and said, 'Where do you live?'

'In that place, Exarchia', which was the central part of Athens.

'Okay, you take that section. You are the commander of that section and your rank is that of a major.'

'Thank you, sir. And who are my second in command and my helpers?'

'What? Are you crazy, my boy?' the professor said. 'There is nobody else. You have to do it yourself.'

'Yes, sir.'

And that's how I became a commander of the Passive Resistance arm of the National Popular Liberation Army (ELAS) in the most vital section of Athens and, may I say, of all Greece.

For true Greeks, the choice was to die from starvation or a bullet. And they all chose the bullet, a lucky bullet.

After that I went back to my room. At the time, you could not trust your own brother, so I did not trust my own brother-in-law and I never talked to him about the Resistance. Gradually we organised small secretive cells — no names, no addresses, just a code name. For true Greeks, the choice was to die from starvation or a bullet. And they all chose the bullet, a lucky bullet.

One of the best street fighters was Melina Merkuri, the daughter of the mayor of Athens, who was at that time forced to serve the Germans. Soon we had one of the most active sections of passive resistance. The Germans were shooting at us, but we were only reciprocating with slogans, placards, flags and songs, as we were not allowed to shoot — not even the Greek scum collaborating with the Germans, the most fanatical and savage executioners of all. It was most frustrating.

The Germans took all the food from Greece back to Germany and, in the winter of 1941, there was a great and sudden famine, with thousands dying, their bodies bloated like balloons with pink shiny skin and millions of lice. People were dragging their dead relatives to the crematorium where there were long queues. Outside a tavern I saw a man pouring wine into the mouth of a dead mate.

Anyway, it was a case of surviving, so I enrolled in the university as a soldier, as they had a lunchtime soup kitchen. But I reached a stage where I could not stay secure in Athens; it looked as though a lot of Germans were after me for different naughty things I'd been doing.

Then my superiors said, 'You've still got guts. We appoint you to another job, as we need good people.'

But that job was worse because they appointed me as a liaison officer between the headquarters in Athens and the headquarters of the active Resistance in the mountains, the partisans. The only trouble was that, to go from one place to another, you had to pass through the German control points on walking trips of 400 kilometres over two weeks. My job was to attend meetings, remember what was said and communicate this with others. On other occasions, I would carry confidential documents, the only consolation being that I was given a small hand gun with only one bullet — to be used as needed.

After fifteen missions I said it was too risky to continue, so they said, 'Okay, we will get you out. But please, one more mission.'

It turned out to be the most complex and hellish one of all — and, as well, the most rewarding one, for which I am still proud. I had to take a group of six well-known old personalities from Athens into the mountains to institute the first Free Government of Greece. It was done, but please . . . I am still shaking. It was one of those stories.

After that I was sent to military school and given a command sabotaging and attacking the Germans. Then Athens was free, the British returned to a welcome with flowers and the National Government returned. But suddenly all hell broke loose. Churchill was not pleased with us as he wanted to make Greece a buffer against the Russians and bring back the King, along with the royalists and the Greek collaborators of the Germans.

After provocation by the royalists in December 1944, the British, with the subterfuge of a joint meeting, arrested all the commanders of ELAS, the fighting arm of the Resistance, and took control of their camps. After thirty days of fighting, we surrendered our arms and were soon at the mercy of the royalists, a bitter tragedy affecting the lives of thousands of Greeks, including mine.

In September 1945, I got a job with the United Nations, a very good position as a welfare officer in a part of Greece receiving all the refugee people and trying to rehabilitate them from different camps. During this period I started receiving offers and pressure from both of the warring camps to join them. Now, not wanting to fight against Greeks any more and, as I had some relatives in Australia, they sent me a landing permit. But the main reason I went to Australia was my admiration for the Australian soldiers I met, particularly the one who had pulled me out of the truck in Larisa. But I never met him.

Finally, I managed to escape from Greece and came to Australia, landing in Fremantle, where I started to admire this beautiful country. I went up to Perth in the bus and I could see girls with short shorts chasing balls and I thought, What beauties . . . What a country! And when I was travelling from Melbourne on the railway to Sydney, the country was full of beautiful big hares. They were really rabbits, but for me they were hares! And I thought, Only Kings eat hare. So I said to myself, Between girls and hares, this is a new paradise here. That was my coming to Australia — I loved this country and I tried to do whatever I could to help a little.

From Melbourne I went to my relatives in Sydney and my uncle, who had fostered my trip to Australia, organised my landing permit and lent me six hundred pounds. So my obligation now was to work in his milk bar. He was an uncle who had been in America in the 1930s and had seen drug stores in which they served milkshakes. He realised that Australia had plenty of milk and that if he started a milk bar in Australia he would make a fortune. So he succeeded with that in Martin Place, where he built a little shed between two big buildings. For twenty years, that was the famous Black and White Milk Bar — the first milk bar in Australia.

Naturally, at that time, I was trying to improve my language, to learn and to improve my knowledge of the country. My best educational experience, and very cheap, was the Easter Show in Sydney, where I could go and see all Australia laid out in front of me. I was also thinking about the future and what I was going to do in Australia, so I investigated the different resources of the country — like opal mining, coal mining, agriculture and so on — and came across information about the pearling industry. Now, I remembered, from home, my mother's love of pearl and pearl shell buttons, and myself serenading the girls with an aria from Bizet's *The Pearl Fishers*. During my research, I read a lot about pearl shell in the north of Australia, so I looked to find out more.

I realised from my library research that Australia was the biggest producer and supplier of pearl shell, which was mainly used for the production of pearl shell buttons. I also realised that the Japanese had small pearl shell, yet they had created a large industry. Let me put it another way: they created an industry with a small pearl shell, making small pearls. So in my mind I said, Well, if those people can do that, why, with the big pearl shells we have, can't we make pearls too?

I immediately thought I could solve the problem. I decided I would try to make pearls in Australia — that

I decided I would try to make pearls in Australia – that would be my future. I did not realise what the hell I was doing interfering in the Japanese pearl industry.

would be my future. My girl cousins wanted me to make a New Year's resolution to choose one of them, but on 3 January 1949, I made a New Year's resolution to make pearls in Australia. I did not realise what the hell I was doing interfering in the Japanese pearl industry.

To understand about the pearl industry, I started to run around fisheries and universities and ask the professors and other experts to tell me how to make pearls. But everybody said, 'Look young man, we know nothing. Go and find out — make one — and come and tell us.' I realised that if I wanted to make pearls in this country, I would have to find out myself. And this is what happened. Many years later I told them how to make them.

Since nobody could tell me anything and I could not go myself to Japan to learn, the only solution was to start and do my own research. So, from January 1949 until 1956, I travelled between Sydney and Cairns, between jobs, earning money and saving so I could continue my research.

About this time, I was fortunate to discover, in the Mitchell Library in Sydney, the monumental book of William Saville-Kent titled *The Great Australian Barrier Reef* where I found a picture of a half pearl he had produced. When I saw that, I knew that my shell must be big, not small, and that I could learn a lot from this man's pioneering work.

One of the biggest obstructions, and the main difficulty I found in my research, was how to stick my nuclei into the periphery of the shell. There was no known glue to do this, yet it had been done by Saville-Kent. I later found he had a trick: a little hole and a tiny little string with a matchstick. Later the Japanese took this technique for themselves, but it took a strange incident to help me find a solution.

One night I was sitting in my office at the Packe Island Pearl Experimental Station when I saw a shadow passing: the shadow of a big tropical rat. As it passed, something dropped onto my working bench, which I soon realised was the soldering iron I had left on the stand to cool. It was not until the next day, when I picked it up, that I noticed that the glue I was using, the resin, was stuck to the soldering iron. I said to myself, Here's something — try that!

So, trying a bit of this and that, I found a way to manipulate the resin to stick the nuclei onto the wet and shiny shell. When I had done that I was pretty happy. I said, 'Eureka — I've done it!' and I have to say that anyone involved in pearl farming today should be grateful to that rat. That rat had done it, not me. Now, I was able to stick my nuclei permanently in pearl shells using a combination of a hot iron and the glue, which I named the 'Magic Rat Glue'.

In a practical sense, for the development of the pearling industry, I give credit to Saville-Kent for achieving this and presenting his photographic evidence in his book, which was published in February 1893. He was experimenting with pearls in 1890, so that puts him well ahead of Mikimoto and all the others. He was also transporting pearl shell from around Broome to Shark Bay in Western Australia. Some years back, in 1983, I was swimming in Shark Bay and I found a very old oyster still alive. I think it was left over from his work there.

In 1901, Saville-Kent presented his work to two visiting Japanese, who then developed his ideas and claimed them for their own. From this research, Mikimoto received a patent for the process, but it was really Saville-Kent who had discovered the process ten years before.

For me, in 1957, finance was non-existent. All I had was a dinghy and I dived from it for pearl shells, with the anchor on a rope, down ten fathoms, pulling the dinghy, getting the pearl shell, putting it in a bag, swimming up to the dinghy and going down again. Meanwhile, the tide was getting quite high and dangerous in the open sea and sometimes this became very risky. I was choosing between tides to do this work.

In that summer, I collected about two hundred pearl shells and I started experimenting and had a lot of failures. But every failure was documented in a little file — every failure was actually productive because it was telling me what I should not do and what I could do. A few days later, I suffered a sudden and painful paralysis of both hands, which still affects me badly and for which I have no explanation. But by 1958, I had produced scores of large half-pearls of magnificent quality, much better than Saville-Kent's, and had advanced the secrets of the round pearl also.

In the meantime, on Thursday Island, the pearling industry became bankrupt in 1958. Now that's a very peculiar story, as I had observed myself in late 1957, when I went out to Thursday Island, that the pearlers there were extremely happy and prosperous after they got a grant from the Commonwealth Government for 120,000 pounds — a terrific amount. They wanted to import Japanese divers because the Torres Strait divers were not good. But the industry was finished only months later, and the blame must go to local operators and also to our own government.

It's a simple mathematical equation. If the Japanese could make good pearls in Australia, if it is good for them, then it should be good for us. To me, it indicates some kind of a conspiracy that, by 1958, we had a bankrupt pearling industry. I was virtually bankrupt myself by then, except that I had a little box of beautiful pearls and samples.

I was running around, telling people, 'Gentlemen, we can make pearls, we can make pearls!' And everybody was uninterested, except Mikimoto, who had heard about my work through publicity in Japan. Mikimoto proposed to join me as a fifty–fifty partner. And that was my great mistake: I

Finally I told Mikimoto, 'Look, I'm sorry. It has been six months that I am here in Japan negotiating with you without progress. I cannot stay here indefinitely, so out you go.'

accepted Mikimoto and opened Pandora's Box. I could not have found a worse fellow.

So anyway, no one in Australia would support the idea of pearls *by* Australians *for* Australia — until finally a company called Associated Rural Industries Limited came in and financed a trip to Japan for me to negotiate with Mikimoto. When I went up to Japan I found a chaotic situation and I found myself against the worst conspiratorial clique.

You must understand, South Sea pearls were the most valuable industry the Japanese had. It is not so today, but at that time Japan was dependent on the pearl. It was an industry supporting 250,000 people and $200 million exchange for the country. It gave employment to many ancillary industries and suppliers, and this was important. And on top of that, the pearl was the ambassador of goodwill for Japan. When any dignitaries came to Japan, their wives would get pearls, which only Japanese people could supposedly produce.

Finally I told Mikimoto, 'Look, I'm sorry. It has been six months that I am here in Japan negotiating with you without progress. I cannot stay here indefinitely, so out you go.' And so I chose another company and it was like jumping out of the frying pan and into another frying pan, but much bigger. I made a second joint venture with this other company, which I believed was an honourable agreement for

Australia because everything was a fifty–fifty investment share — everything . . . marketing, technology, and all under my supervision.

Now, I did not know at the time, but this was against what the Japanese wanted. They wanted to have a monopoly on the pearl at the expense of the Australians and me. And to make matters worse, I was contravening the law because the Australian Government had agreed that pearl techniques must remain the secret of the Japanese and we were not allowed to learn those secrets. All pearls would be exported to Japan and you were not allowed to sell pearls in Australia. What about Australia? They didn't care and all this was very good for the Japanese. And for good measure, the government also had a secret condition, an obligation in which the Australian partner of the joint venture would undertake to stop other Australians and eliminate any rivals of the Japanese in Australia. This was what bankrupted the Australian pearling industry in Torres Strait and it never recovered.

Yet Australia gave me a lot — gave me a secure home, secure work, secure property — and it gave me political protection, but I had no time for politics. Yes, I came into contact with all the politicians like Arthur Calwell and Bob Menzies. They all promised to do something, but didn't do anything, for the pearl. I ask myself, What has Australia done for her pearls? I answer, Nothing.

And did I ever want to go back to Greece? Despite the fact that I was born in Constantinople, Greece is my country —and her heritage, the antiquity, my eight years in the army, protesting in the streets and with the partisans . . . all this is in my blood. So during my fifty-two years in Australia, I have had three trips to Greece. One was in 1969, for three days. On the third day I decided I couldn't stand it any more. They had a military junta. Then I went back in 1971 and again I stopped three days — the junta was still there. I went again in 1994 and this time I stopped ten days and paid my respects to Aristotle and I reported to him on how I made the pearl shell in Australia. He knew all about pearls — he is the father of natural science. He told me 'Good, my boy. Good.' So, yes: I like Greece — I love Greece; it's my country — but still I don't think I'd like to live there. I feel Australian now.

For so many years I felt that I was never discriminated against, I had no one ever call me names. I even joined the RSL — I was one of the boys. I'd have a drink with some of the boys from the (Australian) 6th Division and we'd talk about things that happened. I was feeling absolutely at home.

But suddenly many, many years later, I realised, after all I had done for Australia, that Australian politicians had done nothing for me. I feel they acted against the interests of the pearl, against the interests of their own people, against the interests of the industry that they should have developed for their country. That's what I feel.

I even joined the RSL —
I was one of the boys.

A Chip in Time

The tale of Leopoldine Mimovich

I was born in the north of Italy, which was, before World War I, a part of Austria. When I was only one year old we left and lived in Salzburg until I went to school in Vienna and in Hallstadt (in Upper Austria).

My dad was an interior decorator and I helped him a lot with stencil work and things like this. Then at school I was always drawing and I wanted to be a great painter. So first I was apprenticed to my father. Then, when I had the money, I went to Vienna and learnt painting for three years. My professor thought my work had a lot of sculptural qualities.

'If I find you a place in this school for sculpture,' she said, 'would you go and be a sculptor as I think you would have a good future?' She found me a place in Hallstadt in the school for wood sculpture and, although I missed the first semester, I was good enough. You had to take an examination to get in and I passed it with flying colours. I was there for four years, but that was interrupted during the war when the school was closed down for two years. Then I went back for a year and finished the course and that's how I became a sculptor.

I am sorry to say that I am the only one in my family that has any artistic qualities. My younger brother was quite artistic, but he was killed in the war, which was very sad. My mamma was really against me being an artist because she thought an artist was always hungry, so she didn't help me very much. She wanted me to be a dress designer or something like that — something more practical.

The wartime in Austria really made women take over the jobs of men and so it wasn't unusual that a woman became a sculptor. During the war we had to go for war service. Then, because so many young men were killed in the war, everybody was on the front. The factories were closed and the shops didn't have any men there. The tradesmen were all gone, so women had to do men's work and I think women showed that they could keep the country going. I got a job in an office, which wasn't so bad, and then I had to do a year in a telephone exchange.

When I first went to sculptors' school, it was very harrowing because I was a painter. All of a sudden I got two boxes of chisels — one box for hard wood, the other for softwood — and a Gothic ornament. I had the chisel in my hand and I looked at that ornament and at that piece of wood and wondered, What am I going to do now? I had never held a chisel in my hand before. The boy next to me, said, 'Come on, girlie, you have to hold it like this.' He showed me what to do (the professor didn't show it to me). So at least I knew how to hold a chisel and then slowly I got going. When I got going, I was very slow and scared to cut into the wood.

The professor said. 'If you are that timid you will never be a sculptor.'

I said 'But what happens if I cut too much away?'

'Well,' he said, 'we will glue it on from the back.' And that's what we did.

After that, I was more courageous and I got used to the material itself. I mean, from a painter to a sculptor is a big step, but it worked out all right.

In sculptors' school we had to make a design, something we wanted to carve, and we had to model it in clay. When it was finished, we took a measure of how big it was and we got a piece of wood in that size and we had to carve that. It was really quite difficult because when you are modelling clay you *add* all the time, but with wood you *take away*. It is the opposite process, so it is very good for you. You learn a lot.

We were so lucky in Austria. I formed friends in art school and they are still artists in Austria, but they don't work as hard as I do because, in Austria, artists are paid much better than here in Australia. We had quite a few schools for art, especially for wood sculpture, and there were other schools for textile design. When you came out you had your education and also a diploma for your work. I was impressed with those schools. That's what is missing here in Australia, I think.

When I was back home in Austria, every girl was taught to be a home-maker. I remember my mother taught me how to iron a shirt properly and things like that and I learnt cooking. Even in secondary school, we had one day a week cooking and housekeeping and sewing, so every girl was well equipped to be a housewife. But I just didn't want to be a housewife. I knew, from when I was eight or nine, that I would never be an ordinary housewife. I wanted to be a painter — a great painter — but I became a sculptor. Very similar, very related.

I left Austria because I married a Yugoslav officer and he couldn't stay there, nor could he go back to Yugoslavia because he had fought against the communists. That was 1949 and it was very hard in Europe. Very, very hard. My husband had a paid fare to America because my papa had three brothers in Philadelphia. But he was worried about a few kidnappings of displaced people in the nearby Russian zone so we went to the Australian Commission.

Usually you had to wait two months to go to Australia, but after one month we got permission to settle. That's how we finished up in Australia instead of America — it was a very fateful thing. We would have had it easy in America because I had relations there and my husband had a cousin there who was a university professor in Iowa, but it wasn't meant to be, so we are here. Well, I am here; my husband passed away ten years ago.

* * *

In 1939 Hitler seized the country of his birth, Austria and declared the Anschluss, the union of Austria and Germany. One of his favourite calls to arms was 'Close your eyes to pity! Act brutally!' — a promise that he kept with his fellow countrymen. By the end of the war 247,000 Austrians had perished.

After the war Austria was quartered, with the Americans, Russians, French and British all occupying a piece. This continued until 1955, when Austria was once again given its independence and allowed to return to its rightful place as one of the great cultural centres of Europe.

Leopoldine Mimovich brought with her to Australia not only memories of a country scarred by war but also an inherited artistic ability born out of a culture that has always had a deep love for art.

* * *

I didn't want to come to Australia. I didn't want to leave my country but, well, I loved my husband and that was it. My mamma begged me until the last day, 'Don't leave us, don't leave the country.' But I didn't listen to her.

It was a very hard beginning, as I think it was for every immigrant. I had a lot of sickness and I was very homesick. Because I was so homesick I decided to work hard. I had left my country, I left my family so at least I had to show something for it, to show that the sacrifice wasn't for nothing, and so I worked hard.

When we left Austria, we were only allowed 50 kilos each of luggage. Imagine how little that is, when you have to start a new life in another country. My husband didn't have that much because he was a prisoner of war, but I thought I would take the doonas and the pillows. Then we had clothes, shoes, the iron and the cutlery and all those things you need — and you forget how much they weigh. I had a big piece of Linden wood prepared for a 'Gloria in excelsis deo' nativity, which I couldn't leave behind. So I left the cutlery and the iron and I took that piece of wood and my chisels. From that wood, I made my first piece in Australia, which is now on show in the Immigration Museum in Melbourne.

And it has paid off. If I didn't bring that piece of wood, I wouldn't have done the sculpture and then I couldn't have shown it to people at my work. When I think back, our school taught very traditional woodcarving and my professor said, 'When you finish school you can develop your own style.' So when I came to Australia, I did those real chunky European carvings. But it's peculiar. The longer I've been here, the more the landscape and the people have changed me. As a result, my style has changed completely, for which I am glad. It's more unique — it's not like a copy of the old style and my imagination is still fertile.

When we came here I was so depressed, I cried. We landed at Port Melbourne and the port looked silted up and dirty. I said to my husband, 'It looks so dirty here'. And he said, 'Every port looks like this. Don't worry, where we will go will be nicer.' The next day we were picked up and put on a train. It must have gone through South Melbourne, as there were these tiny little houses and I remember someone saying 'Oh aren't they pretty little houses!' But my sense of

There were these tiny little houses and I remembered someone said 'Oh aren't they pretty little houses!' But my sense of art and sculpture wanted big monumental, beautiful houses, so I said, 'It looks poor.' I was really disappointed.

art and sculpture wanted big monumental, beautiful houses, so I said, 'It looks poor.' I was really disappointed.

Then we arrived at Bonegilla. It was in July and it was cold and we all had summer clothes on. It rained for weeks and the mud was deep. We had to go through that mud to get into the army huts. The army huts were made of corrugated iron and they were open on top and the wind blew through. We were divided, the men to one hut and the women to another. We were shivering. Each one had an army bed and one army blanket and that's where we had to sleep. That was our first night in Australia. We were shivering all night. We couldn't sleep because we were so cold and you just heard sobbing in the hut. There were ten young women there. They all cried.

Next day, the men visited us from the other hut. Where they were, they had a little stove, so during the day we went down there and they at least warmed us up. But we had to face that cold night again. Next to me was another young woman named Anna. I asked her, 'Can you sleep Anna?'

'No,' she said. 'I am so cold, I can't sleep.'

I said, 'Anna, what if we lay in one bed and then we would have two blankets and we could warm each other.'

'Oh,' she said, 'I wanted to say that yesterday, but I didn't dare to suggest it.'

So we slept about ten days like this until we got our luggage from the ship, which had doonas and pillows. After that it was all right, but it was not a good first impression.

When I came to Australia, nobody really believed I was a sculptor because I was a woman. When we were in Bonegilla, the Country Women's Association gave us an afternoon tea and one lady asked me what I did in Austria. 'Well,' I said, 'I am a sculptor.'

'What does a sculptor do?' she asked.

'They make things out of wood.'

> Then they wanted to put us to work on a farm there and I said, 'But I am a sculptor. I didn't come from a farming family.'

'Oh,' she said. 'I've got a dining table that needs shortening. Could you do it?'

I said I couldn't.

Then they wanted to put us to work on a farm there and I said, 'But I am a sculptor. I haven't come from a farming family.' I was quite proud that I was a sculptor. I mentioned to them that I was doing figures of animals and people.

'A sculptor!' they said. 'Oh, you can always carve kangaroos on the farm!'

It was a bit peculiar at the beginning. People really thought it was sort of a hobby. They didn't think that I had studied seven years altogether.

You can imagine how unhappy we were and it was so cold. In my luggage I had two masks which I had carved in Austria. One day I went to the office in the camp and I said to the officer, 'Look, we would be so happy if we could go to Melbourne and start working. I'll give you this mask if you could put us on the transfer to Melbourne so we won't have to wait so long around here.'

He took one of the masks and after three or four weeks we went on the first transport to Melbourne. We came into a camp in Royal Park — Camp Campbell, I think it was called. The huts were divided into ten little cubicles and each cubicle had two twin beds and a little chest of drawers so a married couple could stay there. There were ten married couples in each army hut, but it was all closed up and it was nice and warm and quite good.

And from this camp, we had to go to work. We had to sign a contract for two years because we were assisted migrants, so we had to go to the place the government sent us to work. Each girl or woman had an identity card, on which was written 'Occupation Domestic' and each man had 'Labourer'. I finished up in a shirt factory and my husband finished up in a brick factory.

When I was in that camp, I asked the maintenance man would he make a little workbench for me. I gave him ten packets of cigarettes and he made one from jarrah — a beautiful little jarrah workbench. So I started carving in the camp after work and that's where I did my first work. After four months, we found two rooms in Footscray and we moved out from the camp.

We rather liked Melbourne. It was a very quiet city with lots of trees and gardens and we felt much, much happier. At first, people were a bit scared of us — a bit suspicious — but once they got to know us they were very nice, very good people. To us Melbourne was a graceful, beautiful town. I still think Melbourne is beautiful. Although I was disappointed when I first saw that the houses were wooden and that some looked flimsy, I started to understand that the climate was different here and people didn't need those heavy houses. And the city itself had quite beautiful buildings — not as old as Europe, of course, but some very beautiful buildings. It seemed to be a graceful city, particularly Collins Street, which had lots of trees.

Even so, I was very homesick for my family, my mamma, my papa and my sisters, my brother and also for the mountains. I come from a mountainous region and we were always mountain climbing and skiing and here there was nothing for us. Summer time here was spent on the beach and I was a redhead — I burnt so quickly. I couldn't go to the beach much, but slowly I got used to it.

Then I remember that old chap at the factory where I worked as a wood carver. He always said, 'If you are very sad just say to yourself it's my own fault — I chose it', so that was my motto. Also, I couldn't show my husband that I was homesick, as it would have hurt him. It was not easy, but what saved me was my work.

My husband couldn't speak English, so it was very difficult for him. I had to translate everything. Just before he left Austria, he had a stomach operation and in Melbourne they put him into the brick factory to shovel clay. He had the most horrible pains every day so I went with him to the foreman to explain that he could not do that heavy work. The foreman said, 'I know he is not able to do his work and I can see he is in pain. Go to the employment office and tell them that he is not able to do that work.'

So we went there and the employment officer said, 'You stay there where I put you', which I had to translate for my husband.

'What does he mean stay there? — I can't stand it.'

'Well,' I said, 'That's what he said.'

So we went back to the foreman and told him and he said, 'Go to the doctor and get a certificate.'

When we saw the doctor he said, 'That man is not able to shovel clay. It is a recent stomach operation and you can really do damage to your stomach.'

He gave us a certificate, which said that my husband was not able to do that type of work. We went back to the employment officer and we gave it to him. He said, 'Did you think you could get out this way?'

My husband was quite explosive when I translated that. 'Well, I'm not going back. I can't stand it,' he said.

But he had to go back because the police would have brought him back. My husband was only 63 kilos then and he was 198 centimetres tall. We went back and the poor foreman, who really wanted to help him, said. 'Whatever can we do? I can see you can't do that work . . . Look, I am writing a letter to sack you.'

So he sacked my husband and we went back to the employment officer with the letter. The employment officer sent him to Brockoff's, a big biscuit factory. That was easy work and my husband was quite happy. He finished his contract there.

Meanwhile, the government sent me to a shirt factory to sew shirts. I had to sew collars. Can you imagine eight hours sewing collars? At home I worked on that piece of wood I brought from Austria and carved that 'Gloria in excelsis deo' with two angels holding this scroll and Mary and Joseph and the baby in the manger there. Very High Gothic. And it was quite a beautiful piece when it was finished. So I showed it to the forelady in the factory where I worked, and the forelady said, 'Can I show that to the boss?'

I said "Yes", so she called Mr Colgan and showed him my work.

He said 'Poldi, what are you doing here? You do this work and you sew shirts?'

I told Mr Colgan I was under contract and that I was not allowed to leave and I had to stay two years in the job the government sent me to.

'Well, how can you get out of this? It's a waste of time you sewing shirts and you being an artist.'

'Well, the only thing is that you sack me,' I said.

'You're sacked!' he said. 'But if you can't find anything you know you are always welcome back.' So I only stayed a year. That was a funny way to get out of my job.

In the early 1950s, it wasn't that easy for a woman to get an artistic job. After the shirt factory, I went to the employment officer in Footscray. I must say, Australians really were nice to us then and this man tried so hard to get me an artistic job.

He said, 'Could you do designs for stained-glass windows?'

I said, 'Yes, of course I could do that.' So he sent me to a stained glass factory in North Melbourne. I didn't even go in the office because they said, 'We don't employ women.' So back I went. The employment officer tried hard and eventually he said, 'Look, can you carve furniture?'

I said, 'To be honest, I haven't carved furniture yet, but if I can carve figures I am sure I can carve furniture.'

'Well,' he said. 'I will send you to Myer's.'

Myer's had a factory in Flemington for reproduction antique furniture and I was sent there, where I showed them the photographs of my work in Austria. They offered me a trial and the foreman of the furniture factory came and brought me four band-sawn pieces of wood for Queen Anne legs (for furniture) and one master sample. He said, 'Can you do that?'

'Oh yes, I think I can.' So I did those legs in two days and after doing two other pieces, I got the job. At first, I was a bit scared because being the only woman amongst four hundred men is not easy. The head carver was a little old man with a polio leg and he gave me very good advice. He said, 'Poldi, don't smile at the men. Stay serious and don't talk to them. They will try to talk to you, but don't talk to them. Just say "Yes" or "No" and nothing else because it is not an easy position to be the only woman amongst us men.' And he was very right.

I was always very reserved and never did talk with the men. They did try playing jokes on me. Like one day I came and there was a nest of young rats on my bench and they had these artificial spiders on a cord. I didn't scream and Mr Hollingsworth, the head carver said 'What stupid boys' and took them away.

At this time in Australia, a woman only earned seventy per cent of a male's wage. That was in 1952, when I worked at Myer's. I got five pounds while the men got nine pounds. I had been there about one year when the department manager came past me. He was a very nice man and I said, 'Mr Garten, can I please have a word with you?'

'Yes, Poldi,' he said.

I said, 'Mr Garten, do you know I am being paid like a cleaning woman?'

'What do you mean, you are not the cleaning woman — you are a wood carver here.'

'Yes,' I said. 'But I get the same money as a cleaning woman. The men get nine pounds and I get only five pounds.'

'Yes, yes, Poldi, you are right,' he said. 'From today on, you will get the men's wage.' And I think I must have been one of the first women here who got a man's wage.

When I left Myer's I already had quite a few commissions and so I could start on my own. I worked sometimes until two or three o'clock in the morning and, well, I was young then and I produced many things in many churches and convents and monasteries.

At about this time, there was an architect who wanted the Stations of the Cross. He said 'Do you think you could do them?' But I could see he didn't want to give me the job. 'Oh yes, I could, but if I do the job, I do my own designs and that is it — I would not copy anybody else's.'

Then he said 'But how do I know what you will produce?' Then my husband said in his best English (and he

I said, 'Mr Garten, do you know I am being paid like a cleaning woman?'

was very proud of me), 'Mr Ellis, my wife will do the Stations of the Cross. If you like them, you can take them. If you don't like them, you don't have to pay a penny.'

I worked for five months on them and when they were finished, we rang Mr Ellis the architect. He came and we lined them up in a little bedroom. He went from one to the other, to the other, to the next one, but didn't say a word. I whispered to my husband, 'He doesn't like them.'

'Oh, shoosh,' he said.

When Mr Ellis was at the fourteenth, he turned around and looked at me.

'I never thought you would be such a good artist,' he said. It was a nice compliment.

After that, the Anglican and the Orthodox Churches approached me to do things for them. At this time, they had to import these things from Europe and mine were different, simpler and perhaps more aesthetic. They generally liked my style and that's why I got so much work. It was also probably cheaper than the imported work.

When I worked, my husband stayed at home and did the business side for me. I told him that he could make the prices and I'll do the work. So that worked out very well. I was scared to charge, but he had no scruples about that and said, 'Good work should be paid for.' But it is very hard for a man if the woman is a breadwinner — that's why I let him handle the money: so that he would not feel bad. For me, my work was my life, so it was not a chore for me. I loved doing it. I loved it much better than housework. He was really good. He did the vacuum cleaning, he did the ironing and, except for the cooking (which I did), he helped me a lot in the house. I would come up to the house from my studio in the backyard, tired after working all day, so he should have done his share too.

Well, it was a time when it was not very usual to have a

husband helping in the house and I had to promise him I would never tell anybody! He was a very good man, really, but he was proud and he did not want his friends to know that he helps his wife in the house, so I never told anybody. Now he's dead it doesn't matter, but I would have never told anybody at the time.

When I came to Australia, I joined the different art societies. There were only three professionals I knew — the others were hobbyists — but there were a few quite good artists amongst them. As a sculptor, you lead an isolated existence because you have to work alone. You can't just chat and work at the same time. It's difficult.

When I came to Australia I had no idea what wood to use until I went to Myer's and worked there for five years. The most beautiful wood is Huon pine, which only grows in the Huon Valley in Tasmania and is from 2000 to 4000 years old. Can you imagine? It was there before Christ. It is the most amazing wood, but unfortunately it has been used for fences, for firewood, even for boat building and now it's gone.

I still have some Huon pine in my shed, left over from so many of the big things I've done in it. I did a life-size St Francis Xavier for Xavier College in Melbourne. I did an over-life-size St Gregory the Great for St Gregory's Church in the Melbourne suburb of Doncaster, all in Huon pine.

I think when life is rough and you go through awful stretches, then your art somehow helps you. I was very close to my father who really wanted me to be an artist and when he died, I was so heartbroken I couldn't concentrate. I couldn't work and my husband got really worried about me. I was so sad I just cried all the time. I had never been so unhappy since I left Austria and as I didn't see my father again after I left, that made it worse.

Then one day I started to carve the figure of grief. It's now up in the gallery, but when I finished it, I felt like a stone had fallen from me and that my daddy was pleased that I finished and had said, 'Be free.' It helped me a lot and helped me in my grief.

I think a real artist can only live with his work. It really takes over. You know, when I am alone in the studio, I talk to 'them' and I pat them and say, 'Oh, you be good, behave!' It's nice. They become part of you. It is very hard when they are finished and you talk to them and then you have to give them away and it's like you give your children to somebody. It's not the money you want, it is just you really hate giving them away.

I had quite a collection of my work here and I was once very ill. I had a heart condition and a collapsed lung and so I gave the whole collection to the Kew Council for the Alexandra Gardens. I saw children and people come and enjoy them and I sometimes get letters from people thanking me. So in a way I miss them, but in another way they give a lot of pleasure.

When you are here in Australia, you think you have given up so much and ask yourself why you did it. Then you go back to Europe and you see that Australia has given you a lot. You can't even grasp that people worry about stupid little things — they are so narrow minded — while here, in Australia, we wouldn't even think about it. Australian people are good. When somebody is in trouble they try to help you. I'll never forget when I was sick. They really tried to help me as much as they could. In Europe . . . well, bad luck, you're sick and that's it. I think Australia is a good country. You find that out when you go back and you see how the others are. Very materialistic.

When I came, there were only a few sculptors, but now there are a lot of young ones who do quite good work, have lots of new ideas and try a lot of new materials. They are mostly men, I must say — not many women — as it is heavy work. I think the young people are very nice people now and are very open minded and quite artistic. The standard of culture in a country is always measured by art and building and I even think that the architects have more imagination now. Back in the early 1950s, they put those horrible boxes up everywhere, but now the buildings have more imagination, are more artistic. I think Australia has really come up in the world and I must say that we immigrants have had a lot to do with that. Yes, I think it is a good country. I hope it stays like this.

The art in Australia is really a mixture between Europe and Australia. It's the influence of Europe and yet it's a new concept about Australia so it's a very pleasant marriage, really. I think we do pretty well in Australia, particularly in Melbourne.

When I went back to Austria, one of my very close friends in art school came with her husband to see me. 'Poldi,' he said. 'You come back with your new designs and we'll sell them and you'll be a millionaire here.'

I said, 'I don't want to be a millionaire and I don't want to have my work churned out like this. I am quite happy as I am in Australia.' You see, they have copy machines for wood carvings now and they repeat that into dozens and dozens and everybody's very well off now, but the soul has gone from the sculpture.

You change, it is such a gradual thing — how do you describe it? It's the country that has changed us and we didn't notice it. We became Australians. We didn't want to at first, but we became it. That's what we say also when we go home. Otherwise maybe we would be the same as they are.

I have been here for fifty years. I am glad I am here in Australia now. I wasn't before, but now I am happy here. I feel like an Australian and it's my country. That's all I can say. And I work hard, I still work all day but it is hard work. I will work until I can't do it any more. I am still pretty good for my age, but I won't tell you how old I am. I think every artist works until he drops. It's not work for an artist — it is life. I couldn't imagine my life without my work. That *is* my life.

I think Australia has really come up in the world and I must say that we immigrants have had a lot to do with that.

We Came, We Saw, We Concreted

The tale of Rinaldo Fabbro

In 1930, when I was a young boy in elementary school near Udine (Friuli) near the border of Austria and Yugoslavia, I was given a uniform with a blue scarf, a black shirt and a black hat. It was a fascist uniform. I dressed up and felt strong. I marched down to my uncle's house, which was not far from the school. I marched into his beautiful home feeling like Mussolini. The entrance was a long corridor and at the end was my uncle. He saw me dressed up in this manner, looked down at me and shouted, 'Out of here! Away. Get out!'

I got a shock and started to cry as I ran half a kilometre home to my mother. When she saw me she took me in her arms and told me how my other uncle, her brother, had been killed during the fascist revolution in 1922. From that moment everything changed in my mind and I no longer wanted to be a strong fascist. That uniform, I decided, was not for me and I refused to wear it.

* * *

Benito Mussolini seized power in October 1922 when his Fascists marched on Rome and forced King Victor Emmanuel III to pronounce him premier of Italy. He was very swift in transforming the country into a totalitarian State. You were either with Mussolini or you were against Italy and his ruthless Blackshirts quickly dealt with all enemies of the State.

Mussolini promised to restore Italy back to her rightful place when she was the centre of the known world, a promise he tried to make good by keeping Italy at war constantly from 1935 to 1945. He conquered Ethiopia and then Albania, then on 11 June 1940 the empire started to fall when Italy entered World War II. Italy was still suffering from the defeats of World War I, so it entered a battle it was not ready for, either militarily or economically.

By the end of World War II, Italy was crushed, 160,000 Italians had lost their lives and the country was forced to pay US$360 million in reparations within seven years.

After the war, thousands of Italians migrated to Australia. Rinaldo Fabbro was one of them.

* * *

Well, when World War II broke out, I was supposed to fight but for me this was a problem, as my family and I were anti-fascist. I was called to the army but as I was at the university of Venice studying architecture, my call-up was delayed, which suited me. Eventually I had to enrol in the officer's course in aeronautical construction in Padova, at the airport.

When the Germans occupied northern Italy in 1943 and surrounded the airport in Padova, the German officer in charge promised us in a speech that we would be sent home in a few days' time. I was not convinced, as I had heard firing when some of my colleagues jumped the wall surrounding the headquarters. Trucks from the airport were parked in the open square and the Germans asked where the drivers were. Nobody came forward. The Germans were threatening to execute one in every ten of us if the drivers did not come forward. I immediately felt this was an opportunity to escape and I tried to convince my colleagues to come and drive the trucks. Only one came up with me, as the others were still convinced they would be released — they were taking POWs. So we presented ourselves as truck drivers and were ordered to follow a column going into the city. My colleague was a law student in Padova and knew the city well. As soon as we were outside the airport, at our risk, we went in the direction of the monastery college where he was a student.

Then, while I was driving, we suddenly came into the huge Piazza della Valle, where about thirty German tanks were stationed while the drivers took lunch. They were searching the city for escaped Italian soldiers. The monastery was on the other side of the great open piazza through which we had to pass.

I was dressed only in khaki shorts and quickly told my colleague to take the wheel as he was dressed in the aeronautical uniform. I jumped onto the step of the truck and when we came near I started to salute the Germans. They returned my salute, thinking I was a German taking a truck with a prisoner! We crossed the square and quickly arrived at the monastery, where we were welcomed and given monastic habits!

When I was eventually able to reach home, my father took me up into the mountains at Precenicco, near Yugoslavia, to hide. A few days later Yugoslav partisans came to the village and ordered all the young men to follow them. I quickly agreed to join them, but some of the men who were in hiding were Italian officers who had been fighting with Tito's partisans before the surrender of Italy. When these men refused to join, calling the partisans bandits, one of them was taken into the small piazza near the fountain and shot. Later I was given a beret with a red star, a red scarf and a gun. I soon realised that I would not last long here, as the Italians were new and would be put in the first line against the Germans.

I was not a communist and this was not the place for me, so once again I escaped with the help of my mother, who came on a bicycle to meet me. We travelled by night, she along the roads and I walking through the cornfields, despite the curfew imposed by the Germans.

My father was a wine merchant and delivered wine to the small mountain towns. One of his friends was a priest at Claudinico (Carnia). As I could not remain at home, my father took me to this village, where I became the priest's assistant and taught religion to the kids. I rang the bells on Saturdays and Sundays and in the mornings to wake up the people. Already I was interested in buildings and would ring the bells as hard as I could and run out to see how the wooden bell-tower structure would move under stress. This was my biggest amusement at that time.

Suddenly, one morning, a group of Yugoslav partisans who intended to take over this area entered the village armed with machine guns. They recognised me and started urging me to join them. The priest and villagers saw me with them and became alarmed. The priest spoke angrily, advising me to leave before the Germans put fire to the village.

Once again I ran away and stationed myself in a hay hut in the mountains, where I started to contact young men from nearby villages to join me. There I formed a group of Italian partisans that later became the battalion Monte Canin, forming part of the Divisione Osoppo. We had a green scarf (the emblem of liberty) and were democratic, not communists.

This division depended directly on the British parachute mission working behind the lines. Very brave personnel from the British forces used to parachute down, training and supplying us with arms and food. They were advising us commandants to tell our men to fight because after the war, when we were victorious, everything would be different. We would be free of the Germans and the fascists. There would be plenty of work and plenty of food, and everyone would enjoy the benefits of our sacrifices. We were young, we fought for our liberty, many died, we did our duty.

When the war ended and we were victorious, promises were forgotten.

We were young, we fought for our liberty, many died, we did our duty. When the war ended and we were victorious, promises were forgotten.

I decided to go back to the University of Venice to finish my studies as an architect; but there was a problem, a big problem. During the war I did not use my real name but a battle name, Otto. Nobody was supposed to know where I came from in case we were captured. However, my men found out where I was, where Otto was living and would come to me and say, 'You promised us that there would be work for everyone, progress and prosperity for us all. Look at us now, our houses are burnt, our brothers are dead, some of us have lost an arm or a leg and there is no food, no work. You promised us so much but now we have less than before.'

And I felt bad, very bad. The men from the mountains did not understand that we commandants had been told to make this propaganda. I decided to look around and emigrate because in Italy and throughout Europe the situation was disastrous. It was impossible, there, to help these men who had been so brave and loyal.

When I was young I had heard stories of a second cousin in Adelaide, Australia, and that fired my imagination. Through an Italian friend in Sydney a landing permit was provided and I left Italy in 1949.

My father had arranged for an Italian friend to meet me when I arrived in Melbourne, but my first contact with Australians was with customs. They had me open everything and they looked at everything. And they continued to look at things until finally the friend of my father approached [as was permissible in those days].

Just then, I said to one official, '*Basta!*'

At this the customs officer took me by the shirt and said, 'Who are you calling a bastard?'

This was a big shock for me! My father's friend explained to him that '*basta*' meant 'enough'.

The next day I caught a plane to Sydney and found a room on top of a pub. I remember that, at the end of the

When I first walked around Sydney, as an Italian architect, I was confused because there was no harmony.

first day, I was in my room when I suddenly heard this bell ringing somewhere downstairs and all the people started to hurry out. I didn't know what had happened; I thought it was a fire. Instead the people were obeying a bell that was rung to tell them to leave the pub at six o'clock, which was closing time. This was all very strange to me.

When I first walked around Sydney, as an Italian architect, I was confused because there was no harmony. Sydney was developed with many architectural styles reflecting the colonial influences around the world. Much sandstone was used but marble and granite facades were used only on the dados of buildings.

I remember a building being erected at Circular Quay that is now the Museum of Contemporary Art and for many years there were just the footings. When I enquired why the work was not progressing I was told that stonemasons could not be found. I was surprised, as on the continent there were thousands of men looking for such work. Eventually construction was completed and a fine Art Deco building rose on the site.

My first job was as an architectural draftsman in the office of Francis Feledy, who was commissioned by Lord Nuffield to design a factory for the manufacturing of MG and Morris cars at Victoria Park. On my first day at work I remember that the other draftsmen were looking at me in a strange way. I later realised they were laughing at my mechanical pencil, common in Italy but not seen by them before. The draftsmen were all using normal pencils and sharpening them with a blade and sandpaper.

While I was employed by Francis Feledy I remember that in the evenings I used to stay a bit longer just to finish off the drawings I was working on. One day an Australian came to me and said, 'Fabbro, at 5 o'clock, here you leave everything and go.' And this, too, was really strange to me because in Italy a job had to be finished before you left.

When I arrived in Sydney I realised I was the first and only Italian architect here. This was brought home to me a few times when at six o'clock on a Saturday morning there would be a knock on my door. Opening my door I'd find a tall policeman with a beautiful signorina who would look at me, start to cry and say, 'Oh, no, no, it isn't him. It's not him.' Some young ladies had become involved with someone calling himself an Italian architect and when these girls went to the police the police would go to the embassy (as there was no consulate in Sydney in those days) and find the only registered Italian architect in Sydney, which was me.

In 1950 Clyde Industries, together with an Italian firm, were building pre-fabricated offices and houses for the Snowy Mountains Scheme. A qualified technical man was needed and again the embassy narrowed this down to me. I was offered a job in connection with contracts being executed on behalf of the Snowy Mountains Scheme. After thinking it over I realised this would offer a better opportunity to bring my partisans and workmen from my part of Italy than waiting till I was in a position to do so on my own, as was my intention.

I went to Clyde Industries and agreed to accept the position on the condition that they would agree to bring out workers for all their projects from Udine (Friuli), my part of Italy, shown to them on the map. A week later they called me and agreed to my proposal to bring the men from Friuli.

We were able to bring out 380 men, many of whom had been partisans with me . . . These men and their families are still here today. There are more than 10,000 of them, as they brought out relations and there are now children and grandchildren.

With the assistance of my sister Ornella and my cousin Giordano Pividon in Italy, we were able to bring out 380 men, many of whom had been partisans with me. So I was able to maintain my promise. These men and their families are still here today. There are more than 10,000 of them, as they brought out relations and there are now children and grandchildren. Most of them have become happy, good Australian citizens.

In Italy I was trained in concrete because there is not much timber or steel, so concrete was used extensively — even for windows and door frames in factories and rural buildings. When I arrived in Australia I saw concrete used only for footings and footpaths. I decided I must introduce concrete here in the same way as it was used in buildings in Italy, so I went to see architects with a heavy box of concrete samples showing pictures of what had been done in Italy and what I could do here. But they were reluctant to give me any work, as they always wanted to see where this work had been done locally. I used to tell them that if they did not give me a job they would never see it! So for a long time I was like a concrete salesman!

For me it was very important to continue, as it wasn't just a job but a family tradition. My training in concrete was not only in university but also with my grandfather. He was a concrete specialist who had done work for the Czar in Russia. Before World War I, the administration of the Czar had problems with water seepage and humidity in the Kremlin, where valuables and jewels were kept underground. The same problems were found in the Mint in St Petersburg. My grandfather, employed by Ferro-Beton, a firm from Rome specialising at that time in repairs to concrete structures, was in charge of a team sent all over Europe for this specialised work.

I wanted to start on my own when I finished working with Clyde Industries. To practise as an architect was a problem, as my degree from Venice was not recognised here. Had I become an Australian architect, I would not have been able to build, as the law at that time prohibited being both architect and builder! I chose to be in the building industry, where I was permitted to do the work I intended doing.

I formed a construction company and the first job we were able to obtain was the façade of a four-storey building in Margaret Street. However, we realised we did not have the money to hire the scaffolding, so what were we to do? A friend told me there were some acrobats from Prague performing at the showgrounds. Maybe we could ask them to help us out . . . In fact, they agreed to do the work on the weekends because that was when they were not performing and because on the weekends everything in the city was shut, so no one would see what we were doing. We put poles out the windows and tied them to the floor and these acrobats worked standing on the poles. In three weekends we did the work.

The trouble would come on Monday mornings when people came back to work to find the footpath covered in white cement. The police were looking for the culprits but could find no one and they couldn't understand where the white cement was coming from. We were paid for the job and all was well.

On another occasion we got a contract to build a dam in an orange farm at Kurrajong. The proprietor explained the requirements to me and we did the job quickly in reinforced concrete blocks using my skills in this field. The rain filled the dam and everything worked perfectly — to the great satisfaction of the proprietor, as he had been quoted 64,000 pounds and we did the work for 8000 pounds.

When I was a student in Italy, I had a friend Gianni Avon whose father Gino was a teacher at the School of Mosaics in Spilembergo (Udine). It was there, working with Professor Avon, that I learnt mosaics. Traditional mosaics were sent from Spilembergo worldwide — including, later, to the war memorial in Canberra.

It was tedious work and Gianni and I decided to use mosaics in a different manner. Without the professor's knowledge we crushed the '*pasta di vetro*' (small cubes of glass) and made an abstract design, transferred to a wall with cement like traditional mosaic. We were concerned that the professor would be angry, seeing our work crushing '*pasta di vetro*', which was expensive. However, when he saw what we had achieved he complimented us. Professor Avon followed our new system in his studio — and, in this way, exposed aggregate finishes were introduced.

In Australia, looking at finishes on buildings, I found that ceramic tiles were used extensively, particularly on public buildings and hotels. I thought of introducing here the knowledge gained in applied finishes in Italy.

I made samples and showed architects the idea. In the beginning they were reluctant to use glass chips, asking again where this work had been done before. Luckily, a friend who owned the Cahills Restaurant gave me a job at the entrance of a restaurant in Pitt Street. The work was successful and architects and builders started using my finishes. Skilled workmen from Italy were required to do this work. Later, instead of glass chips, round pebbles were introduced, used as a concrete finish for walls, floors, and pre-cast panels.

In the beginning it was difficult to obtain both crushed glass and round pebbles. I remember going to the Department of Mineralogy, asking where pebbles could be found in Australia. I was told abruptly, 'There are no pebbles in Australia.' So I decided to look for them on my own. Near Gosford I found the most beautiful round pebbles for my work. One of the first examples used for floors in Sydney is at the entrance of the old AMP Building at Circular Quay — it looks just as good nearly fifty years later.

One job in Pitt Street, Sydney, was done using glass chips. To add life, some square gold mosaics from Venice were used. The passers-by would stop to look at this unusual finish. When the workmen were asked about the bright yellow chips they replied that they were gold mosaics. The next morning when I went to see the completed work, all the gold pieces were missing. The whole job had to be redone!

When I was working with Feledy I was introduced to Peter Lloyd, the proprietor of a company representing Nuffield Cars in Australia. His firm purchased a property with a beautiful home on the corner of the Pacific Highway and Fullers Road, Chatswood, where he wished to erect a showroom for Nuffield Cars. Accordingly he engaged a firm of Australian architects. Their submission to the council was refused because the residents wished to retain the environment and the authorities to retain the visibility through the intersection, as there were no traffic lights and the building design was completely obstructing visibility.

Mr Lloyd was desperate, as the property had been

purchased and the council repeatedly refused him a building permit. He remembered meeting an Italian architect at Nuffield and thought maybe he would have an idea as to how to solve the problem. Finally he tracked me down and I told him it was a simple matter to take away the trees and replace them with concrete beams shaped like trees, allowing visibility. When my plan was submitted to council they considered the concept but did not understand the principle of the structure in post-stressed concrete and thought it would not stand up. After various meetings with council, permission was granted — to Mr Lloyd's delight. The job was finally completed, despite much controversy. It caused international interest, as it was one of the first post-stressed concrete structures in the world.

In the early 1960s Harry Seidler, who was designing Australia Square in Sydney, approached me. He showed me the preliminary drawings and asked if I could apply an aggregate finish to the external structure. The building was 130 metres high and I told him it would not be possible to apply such a finish to a tall building — the wind would spray the washed white cement all over the city. I suggested to him to approach the work in a different manner by producing the architectural elements in the factory in pre-cast concrete incorporating the finish, assembling them on site and pouring the concrete as the building was constructed, thus saving the cost of form work and scaffolding. I suggested to Seidler to consult Pier Luigi Nervi, a world-famous engineer in Rome who specialised in concrete structures. Nervi became the structural engineer of Australia Square, using my suggestion.

In 1966 President Sukarno of Indonesia intended to invade the Northern Territory. The Naval Department of Defence approached me to build barges in ferro-cement, a technique using wire mesh in concrete. It was widely used in Europe by Pier Luigi Nervi. Without question I agreed. A contract for three prototype barges was granted, with an additional fifty barges if the prototypes were successful. The barges were to be towed along the rivers of the Northern Territory, carrying tanks with food and ammunition in case of an attack. In ferro-cement, they would long withstand erosion from heat and humidity, while steel would have eroded in no time.

My factory in Taren Point was not big enough to house them, so we built barges in the open, under the trees. It was a huge task as we were not familiar with this type of work. After the first one was built with great difficulty, we learnt to make the work easier. The navy tested the first barge on the Sydney Harbour. Ropes five inches thick were used, to try to pull the barge apart. The ropes snapped but the barge withstood the test without damage and the contract for the following fifty was to be granted. The threat from Indonesia passed and the barges were not needed. We lost the contract but the experience gained by our engineers was invaluable and today many marinas and pontoons that use our principles can be seen throughout Australia.

After thirty-five years in Australia, I decided to become a member of the Institute of Architects. At the examination the examiners were asking me to explain to them what techniques I was using to obtain such excellent results in various buildings, as by this time my firm was the leader in introducing new techniques in building and construction. They say that I changed the face of Sydney, as statistics taken in 1985 show that my company Fabbrostone was responsible for sixty-five per cent of the façades of the tall buildings in this city alone.

Coming to Australia had given me the opportunity to express myself through my work, following the tradition of my grandfather and studies at the University of Venice.

I married an Australian girl from the country and together we had five children. I became an Australian citizen in 1958. Life in Italy would have been very different for me, but in Australia I have had a very happy and successful life.

They say that I changed the face of Sydney,
as statistics taken in 1985 show that my company was
responsible for sixty-five per cent of the façades
of the tall buildings in this city alone.

A Black and White Tale

Victor and Anne Vadiveloo

'I don't know that my father's story is any more or less special than that of the countless other migrants who have gifted this country with their citizenship. In fact, what little I knew of his life before I made a film about him had been told to me by my mother.

'I knew that he was taken away from his family in Sri Lanka and given to wealthy relatives in Malaysia to be educated. I also knew that during the war he was indentured along with thousands of other young men to work for the Japanese forces on the Burma railway.

'He witnessed and suffered the hardships of that labour, escaped, taught himself Japanese, and survived on his wits until after the war, when he was re-united with his relatives and sent to Australia to finish his studies.

'His tale is as much about the Australia of the 1950s in which my father came to live as it is about me hearing his story for the first time and learning about what drove him to become one of the first non-white officers in the Australian Army, and the first non-white surgical consultant in Victoria.

'Hearing, for the first time, this chapter of my father's story, I have felt a sense of pride in him and a connection between us that didn't previously exist. And in that regard his "tale from a suitcase" has helped me to understand not only where he came from but also what he brought and what he's given.'

— DAVID VADIVELOO

* * *

Victor At the age of two I was taken away to Malaya [now Malaysia] by my uncle. I had no say in it. It is the cultural thing that, when brothers and sisters have no children, one tries to help the other. In my case, my uncle (my mother's brother) had no children and, as he was wealthy enough and good enough to educate me and give me a good upbringing, my mother thought it was a good thing to do and I was given to him so that he could bring me up. This is a normal thing in our culture when one part of the family is not wealthy and the other one is: they do these sorts of procedures so that somebody can benefit from what the others would not be able to give.

As I grew up I had no connection with my sisters or brothers, nor my mother whom I loved very much. Though I was not emotionally disturbed, I felt that there was something missing in my life as it is nice to be with people and to be brought up by people. For me, the close contact and emotional thing was not there. As it happened, I had to make my own life, I had to make do with what I had and to make my own decisions on certain things as I went along. This had a great impact on me and made me a stronger person.

At the age of about thirteen, my uncle went back home for a holiday and he sent his cousin from Ceylon [now Sri Lanka] to look after me. Unfortunately, at that period of time the Japanese invasion of Malaya took place and my uncle's cousin passed away, so I had virtually no contact or correspondence with anybody at home and I was left on my own.

During that time the Japanese Army was rounding up young able-bodied people as they had started to build the Burma–Thailand railway and a few of us were taken across by train. They had a constant transport of trucks taking materials and food via Bangkok onto the railway and we followed this route. When we got to the railway sidings, our job was to load and unload trucks and do whatever labouring work was needed. We could see the Australians constructing the railway, but we could not get anywhere near them as they were guarded by Japanese troops. We were lucky, in the sense that we were not under constant surveillance and quite a number of people we saw would escape the area. After about three to six months or so of my being there, a few of us got into a truck that was heading back to Malaya and I returned to the capital Kuala Lumpur.

The Japanese were very strict and you had to obey their commands. When you passed a Japanese soldier or officer, you had to get off your bicycle, bend down low to them and then keep on going. If you did not do so, then they would call you and give you a couple of slaps and tell you not to do that again.

Fortunately for us, the indigenous Malays and Indians were not that badly treated, unlike the Chinese. The Chinese had a bad time; to make an example, a few of them had their heads cut off and stuck at a prominent junction to indicate that if you did not follow their rules, or if you carried out any subversive actions, then this is what would happen to you. It was quite frightening, not having seen a beheaded person before.

Shortly after the occupation of Malaya, the schools were all closed, so there were no education facilities available. However, the Japanese had established schools, so I had the opportunity to enrol myself in one of the schools in Kuala Lumpur and learn Japanese. I attended for about six months, during which I stayed with a cousin who lived in Kuala Lumpur. Finally qualifying in Japanese, I became an interpreter.

During the British occupation, the whole of the Malayan railway system was run by Sri Lankans, so I had no difficulty getting a job. I became an interpreter in one of the departments in the railways and I was the go-between for the Japanese officer who was running the department and the civilian chief. I had the job of trying to convey to the local people what the Japanese officer wanted and what had to be carried out, so it became a good relationship.

During that time I noticed that the only mode of transport was bicycles and I knew that the price of bicycles was pretty high in Kuala Lumpur, and I could buy them cheaper in Malacca. Working in the railways, I had the opportunity to travel on the trains free of charge and I could travel anywhere I wanted.

So, on my first trip to Malacca, I bought a bicycle and took it back to Kuala Lumpur, where I sold it at a huge profit. Well, that was the start of my business adventure and I would do this once a month or every two months. I used to travel to Malacca and buy a bicycle or two. Most of the time I had to ride these bicycles about twenty kilometres to catch a train and put them in the guard's van. This subsidised my income and the extra money was a bonus so that I could go to the pictures or buy a few reasonably valued things that I wanted.

After the war, I returned from Kuala Lumpur to my home in Malacca where I used to live. They were still in the process of reopening all the schools as they were badly damaged by the Japanese troops. We couldn't do any sort of science subjects because all the science laboratories were badly broken and so schooling was a bit difficult. At that particular time I had no idea what I wanted to do. If the war hadn't interfered with my studies I had been planning to do medicine. So I made my decision: 'I will do medicine.'

It was 1949 and, due to the uncertainty of the war climate in the United Kingdom and Europe my uncle suggested 'What about going to Australia?' He was very unhappy about my going to the UK.

I had an associate by the name of Richard Dixon. We had been right through school together and so we decided that we would both go to Australia to do medicine.

For me to enter university in Australia, I had to have some background science education, so I got admitted into a private school in Melbourne and on confirmation of this admission we started to make preparations to leave Malaya.

We had to come by boat. There were only two boats travelling between Australia and Malaya at that time and it took about two weeks of sailing. When I say 'a boat', it was more like a cargo boat, which was carrying cargo between Malaya and Australia and could accommodate about eight or ten passengers on board.

The first port of call after leaving Singapore was Derby and most of the people that I saw on the wharf were coloured people: Aboriginals and pearl divers and construction workers. It was quite strange to see these people in a 'white' country because at that time we had also come to know, or read about, what was going on in Australia — about the White Australia Policy — and we had some information through the media that there was a big court battle going on regarding deportation of an Indonesian lady who was married to a white Australian. But when we arrived in Fremantle, which was our final port of call, things were different: everybody was white — there was no coloured population around the area.

Richard and I made our way to the airport as arranged and we travelled by air from Fremantle to Melbourne. When we got into Melbourne we found it to be like any other city — like Singapore, except for the faces one saw.

Arrangements had been made by the private school for accommodation at the YMCA, which was close to Flinders Street Station. It was quite an experience living in the YMCA. Most of the people were young, but unfortunately, not being exposed to accommodation of this nature, I was quite astonished at how people lived or slept in these places. One night I was woken up by things biting me and these things were hopping around in my bed. I didn't know what they were because I had never seen them before. So the next day I asked one of the white Australians who was living in the area, 'What is this thing that jumps around in the bed?' And he said 'They're fleas.'

I was not able to sleep at night, so I informed my

I said, 'We've come to see about the accommodation advertised in the paper.' She took one look at both of us and said, 'I'm sorry. It's been taken.'

principal at school and said the accommodation was so bad that we were not able to get any sleep or do any study.

He said, 'Why don't you look around and try to get some private accommodation?'

Richard and I got hold of the local paper and found quite a lot of advertisements for rooms available in private homes. As we could both speak English very well, either of us would get on the phone and ring the numbers that were advertised. The landlady or landlord would answer the phone and we would ask about the accommodation advertised.

Not even giving it a second thought, they would say, 'If you'd like to come and have a look at it and you're happy with it, you can rent it.'

The first time, we went to the place and knocked. The landlady opened the door and said, 'What can I do for you?'

I said, 'We've come to see about the accommodation advertised in the paper.'

She took one look at both of us and said, 'I'm sorry. It's been taken.'

This sort of thing happened on numerous occasions and Richard and I clicked to the fact that we couldn't get accommodation just because of our colour. People were very eager to accommodate us on the phone, but as soon as they took one look at us, the story changed. And we noticed this quite a bit while walking along the road, too: people walking on the opposite side would stare at you and their children would call out 'Look at the black man.'

After literally six months of trying to find some place to live we were finally accommodated by a lady in Kew who had a huge mansion that she was using as a guesthouse. She was very pleasant and gave us our first break.

Initially, Richard and I occupied one room and then, as rooms became vacant in the guesthouse, we got some of our friends to join us. At that time, there weren't very many Asian students in Australia. I think there were no more than thirty to forty Asians in the whole of Australia and to see another Asian walking along the street was quite a thrill, you know. There were a few living in other digs and some of them left and joined us. At one stage we had six people living in the guesthouse.

The landlady had set out her own rules and regulations. One of the things she said to us was that we were not allowed to cook in our rooms. Not being used to the type of food that we were being provided, it was hard going. The food was mainly steak and eggs in the morning, sandwiches in the middle of the day, and in the evening there was meat with boiled vegetables. Every vegetable was boiled. There was no taste, nothing at all. We were not great meat eaters and we didn't eat steak or meat first thing in the morning. We usually hated the weekends because we used to get a roast dinner on Saturday, and on Sunday all the meat was cold: cold meat and boiled vegetables, and so on.

We finally came to the decision that we had to do something about it, but at that time there were no Asian stores or places where you could go and buy spices or curried food. Also, there were no restaurants. The only restaurant was the odd Chinese restaurant where most of the food that was cooked was for an Australian taste. So we finally found a store that had Keens Curry Powder — you know, that old Madras curry powder as they used to call it. As this was the only thing available in these stores we bought a few packets. There was no heating in the rooms so we bought a kerosene heater to warm ourselves. We then bought a couple of pots and cooked some curry over the kerosene heater. Occasionally, because of the odour, the landlady would ask, 'Have you been cooking in the room?' We would deny it.

I had to accept the glaring racial abuses that one got. I had to accept this as part and parcel of the way foreign people were treated, and likewise when I went to school. The headmaster informed me that my name, Kandiah Vadiveloo, was too long and was difficult to pronounce. As I was living in a western society, it was better that I had a shorter version of my name. He indicated to me in a condescending manner that 'Victor' would be close to Vadiveloo. I had difficulty at first, but in order to accommodate their difficulties, I said I will take that name temporarily, hoping that I would return to my original name at a later stage. However, that did not happen and the name Victor stayed and has carried on to the present time.

Having got my matriculation I got admission to Melbourne University to do medicine. However, after second year, as they had restrictions there was no space in the clinical year. You had either to repeat the year and get better marks or hang around for one year hoping you would get a spot the next year.

As the Melbourne Dental School wanted me to start in first year again and I did not want to waste another year, I travelled to Sydney to study Dentistry at Sydney University. After a couple of years in Sydney I was able to rent a house in Glebe, close to the university. I had four other boys living with me in the house and all they did, day after day, was go to university, come back, get into their books and study until one or two in the morning. They never went out during the week or even on the weekend.

In order to get them out of their rut, I became President of the Malayan Students' Association and decided to establish some sort of a meeting place. One of the things to understand is that, when the Malayan students arrived in Sydney, most of them were terribly shy as they were well protected at home. They never went out with any girls, as they were too shy to ask an Australian girl to go out to a restaurant or a dance.

I approached the High Commissioner from Malaya and informed him that it was time we had a clubhouse where students could meet, have a cup of coffee, read the papers from home and get to know other students living in Sydney. They could also bring their Australian friends there and establish a better relationship and understanding between the two cultures. The Malayan Government finally agreed to buy a property or to rent a property at Central Railway, on the fifth floor of the Journalists' Club.

In the early days the Immigration Department was very strict on students: they constantly called us to their office to find out how we were doing in their studies. They would also sometimes ask us to present our quarterly exam results or half-yearly exam results to see whether we where progressing with our studies or whether we were wasting time. If anyone did fail, for a year or a second time, they were asked to return home. They were not given an extended visa to stay in the country so there was a big pressure on the students who came out.

I had an office in the Malayan Embassy, from which I conducted my Students' Association business. The Trade Commissioner was very kind to me and I was invited to most of the embassy functions as a representative of the Malayan students. This opened the gate for me to meet a lot of heads from the various departments — the Immigration Department, Foreign Affairs — and I made a point, when students were having problems with their studies or they were being pressurised by the Immigration Department, to visit these departments and ask them to be a bit more compassionate.

Things got a little bit better as time went on and there was no stress being put on these students, for which I was grateful. I had succeeded in doing something. There was not only this pressure but also a lot of pressure being put on the students by own families. When we came out here to study, they expected us to do brilliantly and if you did not do that you were a shame to the family.

When I came to Sydney my guardian, who was sending me money, passed away, but the funds were still coming in for about six months after his death. Then, all of a sudden, the money stopped coming. I was in limbo and I didn't know what to do, as I had to have some money to live and to pay my fees. I understand that one of the reasons for my money not coming to me was the belief in Malaya that I was not studying at the university and that I had married an Australian and settled down, so there was no purpose in sending any funds to me. Here in Australia you had the White Australia Policy; and at home, in my culture, people would not like me getting married to a white person — it was not an accepted sort of thing. Most people who did such a thing were cut off from their inheritance or something.

So I approached the head of the faculty, Professor Arnott, and I said to him 'Look, Professor, I don't think I'll be able to continue my studies as I've got no more funds coming and I might have to give up the course.'

He said 'Leave it with me, I'll see what I can do. I don't like to lose you because you've been a very good student and have good marks. I'd like you to continue.'

A week later he called me into his office and said, 'I have organised with the Dental Board to give you some funds to

I used to go to lectures in the morning, and occasionally drive taxis from about 4 o'clock in the afternoon to midnight and do the rest of my study from midnight until 2am or so, when I went to bed – that was my routine.

pay for your fees and your books, but you have to do something for yourself to earn money to keep yourself.' Professor Arnott was a great man and if it hadn't been for him, I possibly would not have continued my education in this country.

I decided to drive taxis, sat for the taxi exam and obtained a taxi driving licence. This way I could earn enough money to keep myself. I started driving taxis during the vacation time so that I could earn enough money for the following term. I used to go to lectures in the morning, and occasionally drive taxis from about 4 o'clock in the afternoon to midnight and do the rest of my study from midnight until 2am or so, when I went to bed — that was my routine.

When I was living in Kew, I accidentally met, walking down the street, another Asian who was also living in Kew. We talked and discussed things and he informed me that he was living with an Australian family, that he was a Christian and he used to go to a church which was nearby to the guesthouse. He also gave me information that there was the badminton club in the church hall and he invited me to come down with my friends, who were all good badminton players. On our first visit the Reverend met and welcomed us and said that we should come to church on Sundays. Well, we were in two minds as to what we should do. As the Hindu religion had no objection to us praying anywhere, and as it was a house of worship, we accepted his invitation and went up there the first Sunday.

At that time the Reverend introduced us to the rest of the parishioners and we became very friendly with a couple of families. They took us to their heart and, after a certain length of time we were invited into their homes and quickly became part of their families. This gave us our first break into Australian family homes. They treated us so well that all the feelings about the racial prejudices that I had experienced when I first arrived evaporated and gave us great enthusiasm. We thought we had broken a barrier somehow. Also, a lot of the young people from the church invited us to join them to go out dancing, which we had never done before. They even went to the extent of teaching us how to dance. As time went on, by going to the various dances on a Saturday, we met people in different walks of life. When we went out dancing we always went in as a group from the church, so there were no prejudices about the sex, you know — like wanting to dance with a white woman.

When I left Malaya and came to this country, there were no temples except churches where one could go. Because of my religious convictions, I had brought with me my own saintly pictures to which I prayed every day, and more often than not I had to keep these out of sight. The Hindu culture had a great impact on my life. Living in a western society, I had my pictures in my little bag and I used to take them out daily and pray to them and that was how I was able to continue with my religion. Today, there are so many temples all over the country. There are even mosques and Buddhist temples where one can go and pray.

In the Hindu culture, when a child is born, the exact time and date of their birth is recorded. The time is given to an astrologer or a priest and he works out your life and at what stages of your life you will be going through the difficulties, the happiness, and the successfulness of various projects that you might undertake. It is all written in the book and your whole life span is already predicted. As it is written in Sanskrit, I could not read it — I had to have a priest or somebody trained in astrology to read it and interpret it for me. According to this horoscope of mine, I would be going to a foreign country to live and that was where I would spend the rest of my life. It also indicated the success and the sadness that I would have, and it even predicted that I would marry a foreign woman and that I would have four children. So I am a great believer in what has been written about my life. This book has got my entire life, from the time of my birth to my death, and it has also predicted when I will die.

During my stay in Kew there happened to be a chemist near where I was living. We had been into the shop a few times to obtain pain killers for headaches, which you could get over the counter. Originally, the pharmacist looked at us quite confused. After a few visits to the place, he started to enquire where we had come from, where we had learnt to speak so well in English and what our background was. We told him we were students, how we had had an English education and where we came from.

As time went on, we became more and more friendly with him and on one occasion, possibly about six months later, he invited me and a couple of my friends to come over and have dinner at his place. He had just built a new house in Balwyn, which was quite an exclusive suburb even in those days, and we accepted the invitation. We went to his place on the Saturday night. It was customary, we found out,

> The most interesting part of visiting them was their two children, who had never met a coloured person before. One of them quite openly said to his dad at the dinner table, 'Is he that colour all the time?'

to take a box of chocolates for the lady, which we did. But the most interesting part of visiting them was their two children, who had never met a coloured person before. One of them quite openly said to his dad at the dinner table, 'Is he that colour all the time?' His father nearly died of embarrassment.

But the boy went on: 'I would like to be of his colour, then I don't have to wash every day or have a bath every day. I'll never have to wash my neck!'

That is the innocence of a child. The father explained to him that we came from a different country and in that country some people are fair and some are dark but they are all just normal people like him.

When I graduated, although the conditions of racial intolerance had improved to a certain extent, I still had a sense of insecurity about going into private practice, for fear that patients may not come and see somebody who was coloured. I thought they would not like to be touched by a coloured person. When I graduated I had the opportunity to come back to Melbourne, to work in the school dental service where most of the treatment was for children. I thought that, by this sort of work, I would not only provide a service to the children but also try to educate them while they were being treated by somebody who was coloured. And I enjoyed working with the children because they had no inhibitions.

In some areas where I worked, the fathers of the children were very kind and very good to me. They would take me for a drink and the fisherman would get a sack and put a dozen crayfish in it to bring back.

They looked at you strangely because of your colour, but they accepted you and were happy to be treated by you.

At the time when I was in the school dental service I also had to travel to the country, where I did a lot of work on school children, and it was very difficult. Here, bigotry and racial intolerance existed to a greater degree than in the city at that time. However, in some areas where I worked, the fathers of the children were very kind and very good to me. They would take me for a drink and the fisherman would get a sack and put a dozen crayfish in it to bring back to Melbourne. You see, that's how good some people could be. So you get the intolerant people and the tolerant people who can accept you. It gave you so much joy that people appreciated what you'd done for their children and in response they wanted to show their kindness.

Anne Well, I first met Victor when I was invited to go to a function at the Malayan Students' Club. I hadn't met any Malayan students at that time. A friend's brother was befriending some young students who were very shy and he asked if I'd go. I remember all night people kept saying, 'Where's Victor?' And I was thinking 'Well, who's Victor?'

'Oh, you know. He's the president.'

I got sick of everybody saying 'He's gone to get some girls', as I was very prudish and I thought, Well, what sort of person must he be?

Then a lift came up and when the lift doors opened, it was like something out of a film. Out stepped this absolutely sensational man with three or four girls he'd found. It was as if a god had arrived and all the tales I'd heard in the previous hour were true. I don't think I saw anything reasonably after that.

When I first met him, I was only nineteen and in my family, of course, we had never had any curry. He invited me to his house and there was a cauldron of meat curry with bright red gravy (I didn't understand the significance of red chilli because I'd never heard of it) and a cauldron of rice. No vegetables, nothing subtle. And because I loved him so much, or thought I was in love with him, I never said anything about the food. I just tried to eat it all. My sister took one gulp of curry, rushed to the sink and got six glasses of water which she put in front of her.

Vic used to be really worried about the young Malayan boys who were only eighteen or nineteen. They just sat in their rooms and didn't meet any Australians, and in winter it was cold. Vic would get stressed that they were not having any sort of inter-cultural experience, so he used to try to get them involved with Australian families. One of these was a beautiful young man named Bala, who stayed with us and was very, very dark. I remember just feeling heartbroken one night when he was going out to visit and he asked me if he should take chocolates to give to the hostess. I said, 'Well, that's a really nice thing to do.' Then he said, 'Well, then the children mightn't be so frightened of me.' And I nearly cried, just to think what a hurdle it was for him. Vic was encouraging him to go out, but in his own heart he was petrified that he would be rejected by the children.

With regard to racial intolerance towards us as a couple,

We had four children but we never had holidays or anything because he just studied. I remember saying to him that the only letters he should have after his name were GUTS.

I don't think I felt it as much. There was one incident when we were on Wynyard Station in Sydney. I must have had my arm around him and we were close together, and suddenly this older man came up and hissed into my hair, 'What about the children?' I was absolutely shocked because that was the way, when it became obvious that we might get married, that people voiced their concerns. I believed that any children who grew up with confidence, and who were loved, would find a place; if they didn't, it didn't matter what colour they were.

Even before we were married, we were determined to have an experience of what this culture was like and, no matter how hard that was, we were confident. Vic never sought out people of his own culture and I remember him saying, when he was in the Australian Army, 'I make friends with people, with good people. I don't worry what rank they are.' And, in a way, I think that he has made friends with people no matter what culture they are. I think the good thing was that Vic attracted lovely people, and lovely people looked after us.

Vic had a lot of courage. I can remember when he became a surgeon, after being a dentist, and we had four children, we never had holidays or anything because he just studied. I remember saying to him that the only letters he should have after his name were GUTS, because he is very,

very strong and very determined and it took a long time to see what the cost of that was to him.

Victor After being in the school dental service I joined the Australian Army and did service in Malaysia, Singapore, Borneo and Vietnam. During this period of eighteen years I studied and became a facio-maxillary surgeon. I was also a consultant at two public hospitals. Due to the nature of my work I had some disappointments and I paid my price for it. I lost my relationship with my children because I used to go out at about 7.30 in the morning, while they were all asleep, and sometimes I didn't get home until 11pm, when they were in bed. One doesn't see this when one is pursuing a career. With the demands of the type of work that I did, I sometimes needed to be at the hospital at 2 or 3 in the morning to do a case. Career-wise I achieved a great deal of satisfaction, but during the process I didn't get to know my own children or form a close attachment to them. I wasn't able to play with them or take them anywhere because I was so busy with my work.

As I grew older and my work load decreased, and as I became a senior consultant and a surgeon, the hack work was done by the registrars. So I had a little more time to myself and that was when I wanted to have more rapport with my own children. But they were no longer coming to me for anything — not even discussing anything with me. And that hurt me a bit. Well, it still does. But my only consolation to them was that I had given them a very good education and provided them with all that they wanted. They have been excellent students and have graduated into various professions.

I came here to further my education. The amount of racial intolerance that I found made me go on doing what I had to do, what I came here for. I wanted to fight any racial prejudice that existed. But on the other hand, I was also terribly arrogant and had a superiority complex because I felt that I was so well educated, better than most of the Australians — or the white people — in this country. I felt I had nothing to be subservient about — to anyone, in any fashion. I was able to stand up to them, I could talk to them and argue with them and I maintained that same attitude throughout my life. In my own mind, I felt superior to the white person. That gave me great strength to fight the prejudices that existed in this country.

As I grew older and my work load decreased,
I had a little more time to myself and that was when
I wanted to have more rapport with my own children.
But they were no longer coming to me for anything –
not even discussing anything with me.

'We're going skiing tonight'

The tale of Sasha Nekvapil and Frank Prihoda

In the 1930s the world thought that Hitler was on a mission to repatriate all German-speaking people. He alleged that the Sudetenland was the last territorial claim he had to make over Europe. The Sudetenland was a part of Czechoslovakia's territory and with the signing of the Munich Agreement of 1938 Hitler gained one-fifth of the landlocked nation in the heart of central Europe — together with 800,000 Czechs, over three million people of German descent and virtually all of the industrial engine that powered Czechoslovakia.

After the crippling Munich Agreement was signed the Prime Minister of Britain Neville Chamberlain declared that the deal had secured 'peace for our time'. The years that followed were anything but peaceful. Not too long after the Munich Agreement was signed Hungary and Poland helped themselves to parts of Czechoslovakia and then in 1939 Hitler took the rest of the country. The German occupation brought very little to Czechoslovakia, apart from death and misery. Over 250,000 Czechs were killed during World War II.

At the end of the war the struggle for control of the country began between the returned government in exile and the communists; a battle that President Benes lost in 1948 when the government was mostly made up of communists. Soon after the communist takeover, life in Czechoslovakia changed from bad to worse. The communists started to control all business, schools, churches and industries and the secret police started hunting out 'undesirables'.

Soon after this, Sasha Nekvapil and her husband Karel, together with Sasha's brother Frank Prihoda, made the most important decision of their lives: to escape.

* * *

Sasha I was born in Prague, a city of one million people at the time. We were a very close family, but my father, who was a business man, died when I was seventeen and Frank was fifteen. When my father died, my mother had to take over the business, which was the export of artificial flowers. My brother had to leave school and go with our mother to work in the business, which was sad because he was a good scholar. My life as a child was very happy in Prague. Prague was a lovely city, as you know. Everybody loves Prague and all the churches are lovely to look at and it's not too big to get out of.

About twice a year we used to go with the family to ski. Anyway, most of the skiing consisted of walking from one hut to another to visit or for afternoon tea — mainly blackberries and cream or blueberries and cream — so we didn't do much skiing. But I did start skiing seriously when I was about fifteen because my girlfriend had an older brother who was a champion and I had two older cousins who were ski champions, so I was allowed to go away for a night with them. And that's how my skiing started.

I was ambitious and I wanted to ski well. When I was in the first race (I think I was a junior) I came third and I was outraged that I didn't win, because I was quite sure I was going to win. And that was the start of my racing. I continued after the war because during the war there wasn't much skiing. The main mountains were part of the Sudetenland and we had no access to them, so we could ski only in the smaller mountains, which we did up till 1940. But after that there was hardly any skiing at all. We were mainly bicycling during the war, because there was no petrol for cars. We could get away to the countryside for the weekend on the bicycles.

Frank In 1939 I was working in my father's business, my father having died in 1937. Other than that, I was engaged in athletics and running and I took up skiing and ski racing due to the influence of my sister, her friends and my cousins who all were engaged in ski racing.

Sasha The war broke out when I just started competing and there were no more races till 1946.

Prague was very sombre and low key during the war because the Czech government was in exile and the Germans were everywhere. The Germans were our rulers: they commanded everything and everybody and they were in every office in the land. And of course everyone was anxious about bombing, but Prague wasn't damaged much.

Frank Well, the German occupation affected us all very much because it deprived us of our freedom. Czechoslovakia prided itself on being a democratic and free country and it was probably one of the few in Europe at that time. The Germans . . . of course, they're oppressive and we had to toe the line in all respects; do as they wanted us to do, obey the economic and political laws, eat as little as possible and drink whatever you could scrounge on the black market. That was the overall effect, but I cannot say that I personally, or my family, suffered very badly.

Sasha Skiing started again after the war. I was part of the first international race in Switzerland where the Czech team was invited. We were over the moon because after years of war, when there was nothing of the luxuries and nothing of the main staples either, suddenly we were in Switzerland where there were bananas and oranges and chocolate and we loved all of that. And it was a lovely race. Everybody who finished the race received a Swiss watch. It was great.

I still have that watch somewhere, but it doesn't work.

I got married in 1945 and moved to another town. My husband was very understanding and he liked me racing because he was a skier and raced at the club level himself. He became an official of the ski federation and went with us when we went ski racing abroad, to Austria, Switzerland and France. I only had those three years racing between 1946 and 49. As racers, we didn't have a high standard of racing and were not very good technically. We didn't have enough training or trainers to help us. We were just daring and were the best in Czechoslovakia, so we were sent. And since I had been champion for three years running I was automatically selected for the 1948 Olympics. I didn't have to do anything to prove myself because of the title. And those who were second and third came into the team as well. And that was our team: three girls and lots of officials.

We mainly trained by being in the races. Immediately before the Games in St Moritz, I won a race and then a week later the Olympics came and I didn't win. So that was a great disappointment to everybody but not to me. Well, I didn't expect to win against those good skiers, the Swiss and the Americans — although I did all right and got fourth place in the combined slaloms, so that wasn't too bad.

St Moritz was a very fashionable place and was very glamorous because it had beautiful big hotels where the Hollywood film stars went and we were mixing with them. It was very nice for us — a once-in-a-lifetime experience. We were invited to tea at *the* Palace Hotel with Norma Shearer, who was a big Hollywood star at the time and was a skier as well.

In 1948, when the communist putsch happened in Czechoslovakia, we were not happy with that and decided to escape to the free world — anywhere that would have us. First we arranged with friends to flee in a small plane. Our first try was aborted because it rained and the field was soaked, so the plane couldn't take off. The second time we tried, the pilot was arrested the night before, so that was out.

Frank Under the Germans, the oppression was by foreigners, by people nobody liked. We Czechs were all against the Germans. Now, under the communists, though the system was similar in reality, the Czechs were administering it. The problem was that part of the nation was pro and part was against, so you never knew where you were and what you were up against. Under the Germans we didn't live in fear, trembling every night but beginning in February 1948, when the communists took over the government completely, we were living in fear of the future. That was the fear in those days.

Myself and my sister, and the family for that matter, were not considered highly by the communists. We were bourgeois. We were, so to speak, 'enemies of the people'. That was the theory. It affected the business very much, of course. I made a decision almost immediately after February 1948. I said, 'I'm not going to stay here.' And I proclaimed it publicly in front of people. I think it was Easter time of that year when I said in front of a few friends, 'We all have to get out.' And they said, 'What? Why should we?' Some of them didn't say anything.

I said, 'Well, you're going to . . . you can't exist here.'

And they said, 'We existed under the Germans', to which I said, 'You existed under the Germans, but you won't exist under the communists.'

And so my decision was taken then. Later in 1948, when the business was nationalised, it only confirmed my desire to get out. I spoke with the family about it. I spoke with Karel and Sasha and we started trying to concoct some schemes of how to get out of the country, to get the exit permits or to organise some illegal escape. But everything was in vain. Under the illegal schemes people promised you the earth, but they usually took your money and, once they got you to the border, would dump you. And the sums of money were enormous, so I said to family, 'No I'm not going along with that — we'll do it under our own steam.'

Our escape was concocted over the summer of 1948. With the help of friends in Southern Bohemia, we recognised a route that could get us into Austria, but that route in summer involved swimming across a lake. There was an area where there were lots of man-made lakes and this particular one had a very long arm that was only about one hundred and fifty metres wide. So we swam across and found a path, along which we walked into Austria. Here we made contact with a forester who was willing to receive us if and when we did escape.

Now that was the summer, but everything takes a long time to ripen. Then in December of that year, the winter, the girls' ski team was allowed to go and compete in Switzerland. As Sasha belonged to that team, we decided that she would remain, never to return home, and Karel and I would seek our own way across the border. We then organised a lot of secret code words and things like that beforehand.

Sasha We arranged that I would go in the next race abroad, which was in Switzerland, at the end of 1948 and my husband and my brother Frank would both ski out across the border on their cross-country skis. After my race, when the team were about to return by train from Zurich, I just stayed there at the platform and didn't board the train. Luckily I had two friends who knew all about it and threw out my luggage on the other side of the train. For me it was a very easy, very luxurious way of escaping. The team leader said, when the whistle blew, 'Hurry, hurry let's go.'

When the time came to act we made a telephone call to Switzerland and used our code word to let Sasha know we were ready to escape. And the code was 'we're going skiing tonight'.

'No, I'm not going,' I said.

'Come on, come on. You must come.'

I said 'No.'

She had to go because the train was leaving and the team were already on the train. I kept far enough from her so she couldn't grab me and take me into the carriage. That was a great relief, but after that I had to go to the police. And I knew then that Karel and Frank were walking across the border and I was hoping that they would succeed. I did get a telephone call soon after that they had reached Vienna, which was under French occupation at that time.

Frank For Karel and I, there were two possibilities: to go to Germany, which was very difficult; or to go to Austria, which was comparatively easy. But in Austria, you entered the Russian zone and your difficulties did not stop on the border. They kept going until you got out of the Russian zone.

When the time came to act we made a telephone call to Switzerland and used our code word to let Sasha know we were ready to escape. And the code was 'we're going skiing tonight'. I said that word, but I wasn't quite sure that she understood fully. At that time, all foreign calls were monitored, but nothing came out of it. The die was cast and so we had to do it. So we did.

When we escaped we had a lot of friends in the ski

racing community. One of my close friends was a pharmacist by trade. He was still allowed to drive a car, so he very nobly offered to drive us to the border. In itself, to get to the border was not very easy as there were all sorts of controls; and to go by train took an awfully long time and you are very visible and exposed to the police.

On 15 January 1949, we set out from Prague at about four in the morning and drove in the dark, south into Southern Bohemia, to the area where we would cross the border. At the time, I was sharing a flat with a good friend of mine and his aunt. At the end of the war, they formed a sort of volunteer troop and he was one of them.

One day, he brought home a bazooka. It was very hard to get rid of it and of course it stayed at home and he never did anything with it. So it stood there wrapped up in rags. Then, on the eve before setting out, his aunt came and said, 'Frankie you know that bazooka, I can't have it here. They will lock us all up'. So, I wrapped it up in more hessian and we took it with us in the car and dumped it on the roadside outside of Prague. It sounds pretty simple, but had anybody found it in the car it would have been the finish for all of us. Anyhow that went well, so we drove on.

Because these lakes froze over in winter, the idea was that we could ski over the ice into Austria. But low and behold, as we were passing the lakes, we saw that they were all liquid. They were clear of ice and we thought, Oh God, we can't swim now, but we might have to later. Anyhow, we came to the end of the road, to a point beyond which no cars were allowed to go, which was about two or three kilometres away from the lake. There was some snow cover as far as the lake, so we put our skis on and skied along the road. There we stopped and looked to see if there were any border police around. Nothing moved. Fortunately for us, that particular arm of the lake was frozen over. It was not very solid ice, but it was holding. And we saw some deer walking over the ice and we thought, Oh it's all right, everything is quiet.

So we began skiing over the lake, going calmly. But halfway across, we started going faster and faster. I said to Karel, 'No, no it looks suspicious. We'd better slow down again.' So we slowed down and got onto a secret path in the woods, took our skis off, put them on our shoulders and walked towards the house of the forester with whom we had made contact the previous summer.

The forester took us into the house and was very hospitable and gave us food. We then found that the bus that would have taken us to the main railway line did not go in the winter, so we set out with the forester at two in the morning on a beautiful moonlit night. There was a lot of snow around and it was freezing and the trees looked lovely, like a picture postcard. We walked for about three hours until we got to the railway station. But there, again, we had bad luck: there were Russian soldiers everywhere, and not only that but the six o'clock train didn't go as it was Sunday and we'd have to wait until three o'clock in the afternoon. We put our luggage — our little rucksacks and skis — into safekeeping and went to the village. There we walked around and bought some tea. We didn't have ration cards, though, so we were not sure whether we could ask for food or not. Fortunately, in the tavern, they had some food — bread and lard.

At two or three in the afternoon we walked back to the station and picked up our luggage from safekeeping. But I started feeling suspicious because the railway clerk told us to wait and he walked off. This I thought was not a good sign. Nevertheless, we had our tickets, which the forester had bought in the morning, so we looked like local people travelling.

In those days there were barriers where you had to show your ticket and then you were admitted onto the platform. There was a railway man doing the punching and next to him was a civilian guard. In German he said, 'Where are you going?'

Karel said, 'Oh we're going to Vienna.'

He said, 'And what are you doing in Vienna?'

'Well, we're studying. We're going to the university.'

'Oh yeah. And what nationality are you?' Well, you can see these things by the clothing. He said, 'You're Yugoslavs. Can I see your passports?'

We did have passports, but they were not valid as we did not have the exit visa. He looked at them and he said in Czech, 'I thought so. This is illegal, you know. I can't let you get on this train. I have to report it to my commander. You have to wait for the next train because I have to inform him.'

The next train was at six o'clock in the evening so that was consoling, as he had said, 'I can't let you get on *this* train.' It didn't seem to be very serious.

Then he said, 'Well, I'll have to lock you in.'

So he locked us in the waiting room and there we waited. He came at about five o'clock and said his commander was not back yet and was not coming again today. This meant we would have to wait overnight and be locked in the waiting room which, by that time, was about minus twenty degrees — freezing cold.

We stayed the night locked up in the waiting room of the railway station and in the morning Karel and I saw the commander. After a short hearing and a suitable bribe, we were let go and escorted to the platform so that we could board the next train to Vienna.

In Vienna I had an aunt who lived in the British sector. We got to her, reported ourselves to the authorities and went through a lot of paperwork and registering and so on. In the end we managed to secure a permit to leave Vienna and boarded an overnight train, which went to Innsbruck. Our goal was St Anton, where we were to meet up with Tony Sponar [another Czech Olympian from the 1948 team, who was to become a well-known personality on the New South Wales snowfields] and eventually with Sasha.

So we got to Innsbruck, met up with Tony Sponar and started our business, which was to run a portable ski lift in St Christof, a village above St Anton. In the meantime we got in touch with Sasha, who was in Switzerland, and she started working on the permit for her to leave Switzerland and go to Austria, which took quite a while.

Sasha After arriving in Switzerland, I had to go to the police every day. And every day I tried to get visas for Frank and Karel to join me there, but after two months of unsuccessful lobbying I went to join them in St Christof, where they had a little ski lift made out of Frank's jeep motor. They made a bit of money and we lived in an elevated farmhouse with cows under the floor in the bottom part of the house. The house smelled of cows all the time. I became pregnant while we were there, and then I couldn't stand this smell. It was awful and we didn't stay long.

The last time I left Prague I had to plan to have the basic things that I would need when I escaped, but I couldn't have too many suitcases as the team would be suspicious. So I only had three suitcases, but I had three fur coats, thinking they would be good for selling, to make some money for bread and milk, which we did. We sold everything we had. And leaving Prague for the last time; I thought I would never see Prague again; we were quite sure that there would never be an end to communism. When I returned ten years ago, it was a delightful surprise, so we

> I drove straight to work from the ship, as I had a job lined up. I appeared at the factory on Friday at half past twelve. At one o'clock the hooter went and I started working.

can go and visit Prague again, visit our place, which I did. Oh, it's lovely.

Frank At Easter in 1949 we were fortunate to obtain visas for us all and in May of that year we all got into Belgium. Then, of course, what to do next? The United States was out because there was a quota on visas for Czechs. One day, in the *London Times,* there was a big article about Australia and how they wanted migrants. And so we decided: Let's all go to Australia and to Melbourne because it has four seasons of weather. We always thought Sydney was too hot and so Melbourne it was. Fairly simple.

I came out first [Sasha and Karel stayed behind till the baby was born] and when I got to Melbourne there was a train strike and taxis were lined up by the ships. My first impression, as we drove through Port Melbourne, was of the horse troughs and the horse rails, and on the main street there were even some horses tied up. This was the real Wild West; ah, it's a good country. Then we went through Collins Street and into the suburbs and I thought, It looks pretty good and like a normal town, a normal city.

I drove straight to work from the ship, to a firm who were manufacturing artificial flowers, as I had a job lined up with them. I appeared at the factory on Friday at half past twelve. At one o'clock the hooter went and I started working. In the factory I met many kind people and my boss got me lodging in his mother's house. Then I gradually started getting used to the Australian way of life.

I had some Czech friends there and I went out with some people from the factory. On the first Saturday, I made a date with a girl in the factory. We went dancing, but that was not a great success. And then gradually I got to meet a lot of people playing tennis, but of course the main thing was skiing.

Sasha We lived in Belgium for two years and I had the baby there. Then we set out for Australia, travelled by train to Paris, then by train to Genoa, from there we got the ship. Our passage to Australia was paid by a refugee organisation, so we didn't have to have a contract or pay anything. For five weeks I was seasick all the time, but it was a very good trip and when we landed Frank was already here. He had a big American car and took us from the port the scenic way into Melbourne, round the Yarra, and to his flat. He accepted us in his flat in Kew and we lived there with him for eight years.

Frank We started going to Mount Buller and, through skiing (we had good reputations as Sasha, Karel and myself were very good skiers), quickly made friendships and acquaintances with lots of people. And so we met people from classes who, as migrants, we normally wouldn't meet — the cream of the Melbourne society — and we got into a lifestyle that was very pleasant and agreeable.

Sasha When we got to Melbourne we knew we were going to settle in the snow somewhere, somehow. And so the first opportunity we had was to become caretakers of a club lodge at Mount Buller [in the Victorian alps], which we did and opened a ski school there. But I didn't like to live in that club because it was pretty primitive, so when the opportunity came, we went to Charlotte Pass. I began going every year to Charlotte Pass, which is in New South Wales, near Mount Kosciuszko, to be a ski instructor. That was lovely. It was hard work because I was on my feet all day, but it was warm and the work was just outside our front door.

And that was the only money we had at the end of those seven years' teaching at Charlotte Pass, when we started the lodge at Thredbo. The money that my husband made working in the hotels, as an assistant manager, looked after our needs and the money I made was the cream; and that's what we started with here, in Thredbo.

Frank I stayed in Melbourne for twenty-five years and in 1956, through racing in all the Victorian and Australian races and being a place getter in almost every race, I was selected for the team and was fortunate to represent Australia at the Winter Olympic Games in Cortina, Italy. They had to hasten my citizenship because there was a five-year minimum requirement, and to be able to be entered into the Olympics I had to be an Australian subject. So they added about three or four months onto my stay and then gave me the [citizenship] paper about six months early.

In the games, none of us went with big hopes. But I competed in the giant slalom and I didn't finish well there. I was towards the end. And then I competed in the slalom and, with 112 starting, I came fifty-sixth. That was my result. And it was very hard, very difficult skiing there. But I felt Australian when I was competing, very much so. I was proud of it.

Sasha We started the lodge in Thredbo in 1959 and it was finished by the long weekend in June. We had fifteen beds, so we had fifteen guests for that weekend. There was no snow; that didn't come until August that year. It wasn't a good season for us to start with, but we managed. Our main objective was to pay off our loan.

Back in the 1950s, Thredbo village was much smaller, of course — with about eight buildings altogether. There was another commercial lodge, and they built a big hotel in 1962. There were a lot of other nationalities working here: Hungarians; Austrians; Swiss people; Polish, I think; and quite a few other Czechs as well. I don't know how they got here — perhaps the people drifted from the Snowy scheme. And there were refugees from the Hungarian revolution in 56; that was our builder and his partner.

It was like a family, because there were so few people that everybody knew each other. Summer was very lovely here, idyllic. We had a bit of a summer season because the Continental people didn't like the beach and were used to the mountains, so they used to come here. We had about a two- or three-week season in summer, with horse camps for the children. We were open every day, for the whole year, for many years, until we sold the lodge.

It was hard work in the lodge because although in winter we had a chef or a cook, very often they either left or were sacked and we had various horrible people to fill in. If you got rid of them, you had to cook yourself until you got somebody. Then we had some good ones; we had Tony Bilson for a good part of a season, but we didn't know he was going to be such a wonderful chef as he is. And there were always parties going on somewhere — not for us, because we had to work, but the staff partied all the time. Skied and partied. It was a good life that they had.

We had a good life, too, as we had lovely guests whom we became very friendly with. We used to have a fondue party every Wednesday when fondue was a new thing. Then

I had the shop in Thredbo from 1959 until 1980. I loved the shop because I met very nice people and I dressed them in beautiful ski clothes. My first 'shop' had been just a big glass cupboard in the dining room: when dinner finished, the cupboard was opened and people bought things — that was the start of the shop.

What really set me up was that, during the 1950s, when I was teaching at Charlotte's Pass, I wore red ski pants. They were the only red pants in all of Australia and I got very well known for that. Another thing was my big straw hat, which I needed for the sun. So I had a big straw hat and the red pants, and these put me on the map.

Frank Well, Sasha was a trailblazer and an innovator. She had the advantage of knowledge of the European ski fashions and, when she started travelling in Europe, knew the brands and she knew the skis and the boots. And so she put a new spirit into the supply of ski clothes and ski equipment, especially for ladies. I also remember her trademark black pants, which replaced her red ones, worn with a yellow top. And that was very daring, you know, in those days. It was a strong contrast and I think there were a few comments.

Sasha Frank came to Thredbo in 1974. He got the shop here and has loved it ever since. He was an eager trout fisherman and this was why he used to come here every summer. Actually, I think he'd seen Thredbo before we did, on one of his fishing trips.

Coming to Australia, it was worth it to escape. We are happy in Australia and we've had a happy life here. First of all, it gave us freedom to do what we wanted and the opportunity to succeed in what we wanted to do — and a nice lifestyle and a feeling of belonging. Every time I go overseas, which is very often, I'm so happy to be coming back to Australia. We are not Czechs any more; we are Australians now. I think a successful migrant is one who becomes Australian. And we consider ourselves Australians in spite of the accent.

When we first came to Australia we were not terribly happy, because the shock was great. It is a different country, completely different. And it wasn't easy to adjust to all the changes. And for a while we were thinking we would like to live in the United States, because we had some friends there. But after a few years living here, you get used to the countryside, which is very forbidding to somebody who comes from a densely populated country in Europe. It is forbidding driving for hundreds of miles and not seeing a living thing. So you have to get used to it. And we got used to it, mainly because we had such good Australian friends, but it took four or five years before we were completely happy.

Frank For me, Australia meant freedom — that's why I came here. I respect authority, but I don't want to be dictated to. And I don't want to be ostracised by the fact that I was born on a different level than somebody else. These were my objections to my home country.

In Australia I formed a life and I am comfortable living here. And I'm very happy after twenty-five years in Thredbo. I love conducting the business in lovely surroundings with the very nice people I associate with and that's worth a lot.

We paid a price to immigrate, as it is always a sad story, a sad time in your life. You have to give up your former life, your former family, all the things, all the people you loved, things you are used to, things you knew, and go forward into the unknown. It's all right as long as you are young enough to do it. It's not a good thing for older people to do. I wouldn't recommend it. Young immigrants who have settled in Australia and then, twenty years later, bring their old mother and father here . . . Well it's really disruptive for those parents and they are never happy.

For us, the sad thing was the loss of Karel's family, his friends, not to see them again. His parents both died. Luckily his sister immigrated later on and she settled in San Francisco, but we never managed to see her and she died. Well, this was outweighed by the chance of freedom. As I say, it wasn't such a big price — it was sad, but it wasn't all that bad, and so we gained a new life and started a new life for the family.

Sasha What have I given Australia? I have contributed to the development of the ski industry and of the tourist industry and our contribution was quite good in that regard.

Every time I go overseas, I'm so happy to be coming back to Australia. I think a successful migrant is one who becomes Australian. And we consider ourselves Australians in spite of the accent.

Crocodile Tears

The tale of Ron and Krystyna Pawlowski

In 1939, at the beginning of World War II, Poland was divided in half, with Germany and Russia each taking a piece of the country. The Poles fought bravely but were defeated within a month and Poland disappeared from the face of Europe. The division did not last long: the Germans attacked the Russians in 1941 and seized all of Poland.

Poland was devastated by World War II, suffering widespread death and destruction. Many large cities were reduced to rubble and six million Poles lost their lives. This was the childhood homeland of Ron and Krystyna Pawlowski.

At the age of thirteen Ron Pawlowski exchanged his toys for bombs and joined the underground resistance movement and by fourteen he was an expert in the game of destroying communications. At the age of thirteen Krystyna was sent to a Siberian labour camp.

Their lives did not cross paths until they arrived in Australia. And it is to the chance meeting of this remarkable couple that the crocodiles of Queensland owe their protection. Ron and Krystyna have played a significant role in establishing the crocodile farming industry in Australia.

However, they have not always made it easy for Queensland crocodiles: Krystyna is in the Guinness Book of Records *for having shot an 8.63-metre crocodile — the biggest ever shot; and she and Ron together had shot 10,000 of the creatures before becoming distinguished conservationists.*

Ron and Krystyna's separate lives in Poland are a million miles away from the happiness they eventually found in their Karumba paradise, Far North Queensland.

* * *

RON Born in Warsaw in 1926, I went to school at the age of five and my life was quite uneventful until the war broke out in 1939. The Germans marched into our town on 7 September. My father was picked up right away and shot, as most people were — people like the Lord Mayor or people who amounted to something, those who could be dangerous to the German occupation. We had to watch the execution, during which mother broke down and so was severely beaten. The last I saw of her was when she was thrown on a truck and that was it. We kids, my sister and I, were now homeless.

Krystyna I was born in Krotoszyn in 1927. My father was a school master and we lived in the village of Lebiedziewo, where we had been about twelve years when the war started. First the Russians came and took my father away and sent him to Siberia. After a while, they took us to Siberia as well, but unfortunately I never saw my father again. Apparently he returned to Poland after the war but we were in Africa by then.

Ron After the death of our parents, my sister and I parted for safety reasons. I thought she would be safer without me — I was thirteen then and, as a lot of kids were being rounded up, I went bush.

I thieved potatoes at night from the field, ate them raw because I couldn't cook as fires can be seen from far away. Well, I survived the winter, became a partisan at the age of fourteen and a half and started making hand grenades — it became a personal battle with me. I had a debt to pay and

I joined the partisan movement but I never belonged to them. I was a loner: I never believed in joining any organisation because when a unit is ordered to surrender you must surrender.

none of my hand grenades ever failed. I made them not out of steel but out of cement, mixed with nuts and bolts and glass and everything, and they worked perfectly. Then I moved into Czechoslovakia — or, to be precise, into Slovakia: a separate territory. I joined the partisan movement but I never belonged to them. I was a loner: I never believed in joining any organisation because when a unit is ordered to surrender you must surrender. I myself was not going to surrender. I blew up bridges. I blew up power poles, telephone poles.

I was just eighteen when I was arrested in Slovakia. It was simply that I was unlucky because it was a road patrol and I was called upon to produce my identity papers, which I didn't have. When I went on a mission, I had a gun with me and explosives. When I completed my mission I threw the gun away and walked away unarmed. That was how I survived. If I had had a gun at that moment I would have been dead.

Anyway, I was arrested and handed over to the Gestapo. They tried to soften me up but failed and a few weeks later I overpowered a guard and made for the woods.

The German patrols in 1944–45 no longer entered a forest because the partisans knew every single tree and the Germans were strangers there. Anyone who entered the forest never came out, so I was pretty safe there. Those were tough days and already I had a lot of friends then, especially amongst the Hungarians and the Slovak partisan units. I made it a specialty to collect morphine off the German dead — up to two or three grams of morphine. At night I used to crawl out and administer injections to people who had, you know, half their insides blown out or legs torn to pieces. And I also learnt how to administer an injection to help a man die.

Those were horrible days. I then made my way towards the American lines and I was almost literally killed by kindness. I was just a bag of bones, three-quarters starved, and they gave me this fat-rich food right away and put me into a military hospital because when I first made contact with the Americans I gave them details of German positions. I had drawn them on paper as I crossed the German front. It was no child's play to cross a battle line but I had some experience, years of experience. Well, they were very grateful because it shortened the time of battle and probably saved many American lives.

And at war's end I assisted the British Army in Lübeck, Germany, in establishing a basic medical care centre for the Polish displaced persons.

Krystyna After two years in a Siberian labour camp I was released and forthwith made my way through Kazakhstan, Usbekistan and Turkmenistan into Persia, where I was taken care of by Polish Army units in training for battle in North Africa. In Teheran I attended a Polish school until transported to a Polish refugee camp in what was then Tanganyika, British East Africa. I met my first husband there, the man with whom I had three lovely children. Then came the Mau Mau uprising and in 1950 we fled to Australia.

Ron After working with the British Control Commission for Germany, I joined the British Merchant Navy, as the third radio officer, and was receiving nine pounds sterling a week. The third radio officer always does the dirty work and is put on night shift because the senior ones want day shift and to sleep at night, but I was happy, I had three changes of whites every day and a great life, but I realised that I wasn't going to spend the rest of my days at sea.

One day my ship, the *Oxfordshire*, pulled up at Fremantle. Customs and immigration came on board and looked through the ship's papers. They must have noticed my record — I spoke five languages and had done welfare work — because they came to me and said, 'Look, we are about to receive a large number of immigrants from Europe and you are just the man we need.'

To cut a long story short, they talked me into resigning from my job. The captain was very good about it, he was lovely. He said, 'Well, you're a young boy. See what you can do in Australia.' That was very, very nice of him.

I moved into Cunderdin in Western Australia, which was then a large migrant holding centre, but I soon tired of that. I had to translate petty complaints and perhaps that was the worst — it was embarrassing. I didn't want to quit the Commonwealth Public Service, though, so I applied for a position in the Department of the Army, where I became a stocktaking clerk at No. 5 Base Ordinance Depot in Nungarin.

Krystyna When we arrived in Australia we first went to Coolgardie in Western Australia. They were sending people everywhere, wherever there was a job. Then we were sent somewhere closer to Perth and we found a house in Perth and moved in. We had only one room at first. That was not good enough so I found a bigger house — there were six rooms and a kitchen and it cost me ninety pounds to lease the house. I couldn't afford it, but I had quite a few couples wanting to live there and I had two rooms, one (the smaller one) for my children and one for me, and I rented out the remaining four rooms.

Ron The army was all right but I soon tired of that, too; I tired of everything that I could do well. Then, one day, I heard about gold mining. I looked at the map of Australia on my wall in a very little office and I worked out that there was something like 30,000 coast miles around Australia so I asked myself, What am I doing in this little cubby hole?

I quit and bought myself a Whippet utility (for the princely sum of forty-five pounds), a few boxes of gelignite and mining equipment. For ten shillings I bought my miner's right and went gold prospecting. I went to the Murchison–Gascoyne area of Western Australia, where I didn't do too badly. I never struck it rich, but I wasn't short of a pound, so I was doing all right.

Every year I used to travel in to Perth for supplies and I made the most of it. I always stayed a week in Perth, went to the dentist and the doctor — that sort of thing. Because I worked on my own, I had to be healthy. If you have an accident, well, you're on your own — that was it. If a log fell on you or something like that, you were finished.

At that time, in 1955, I had a doggy. Before, when I went to Perth, I'd stay at the Savoy Hotel, which at that time was the best hotel in town. But it didn't cater for pets so, on my arrival in Perth, I pulled up at a Polish restaurant for breakfast. The proprietor came out to greet me and I said, 'I am looking for a boarding house and I need a room. But the doggy has to be with me and I'm not going to slum. It's just got to be a good address.'

'Well,' he said, 'I know a lady — she's a Polish lady — I don't know if she has a vacant room . . . Doesn't hurt to ask.' He gave me her address.

Krystyna When I met Ron I was already a widow with three children. I remember I was standing in the corridor of my house, with my friend, and Ron walks in . . .

Ron It was 6 o'clock in the evening. I walked through the door and she stood sideways to me at the table about twelve feet inside the hall. In that split second I knew Krys would be my wife — and I didn't even know if she was married or not.

Until that moment I was a confirmed bachelor with

When he proposed to me, I said, 'I like you but I don't love you.' He said, 'I'll make you love me.' And he did.

strong views against marriage for I had seen the troubles other people had. No, never, never would I marry. Krys changed all that within a fraction of a second. I felt comfortable with her. The chemistry must have been right. One week after that encounter, we were married and we have never looked back since.

Krys had had enough of Perth, I of mining. We both sold out and one month later, on 29 July 1955, we embarked upon our journey into a fabulous adventure.

Krystyna Well, when he proposed to me, I said, 'I like you but I don't love you.' He said, 'I'll make you love me.' And he did.

When we packed the car and got in, the suspension springs bent the wrong way; the car was obviously overloaded. We had to leave very early in the morning, so the police wouldn't catch us. It was horrific.

Well, we had Ron and I, three children, a dog and all our possessions — we had quite a lot of things, you know.

Ron I had an ex-army tent (ten by twelve feet), a billycan and everything. We just went east, across the Nullarbor, and then we saw a track going north to the Northern Territory. I didn't know where it went, but we weren't worried and we ended up in Coober Pedy, which was only a tin-shack town at the time — with not too many tin shacks either! We went north, through Coober Pedy and on to Pine Creek,

For many post-war European refugees, the long journey to a new land began with a train trip to the port of Bremerhaven, Germany.

Clutching loved ones, treasured possessions and tiny suitcases packed with personal necessities, an emigrating family prepares to embark at Bremerhaven.

Farewell. Out of reach and soon to be out of sight.
Arrival. An emotional moment in Cairns, 1956

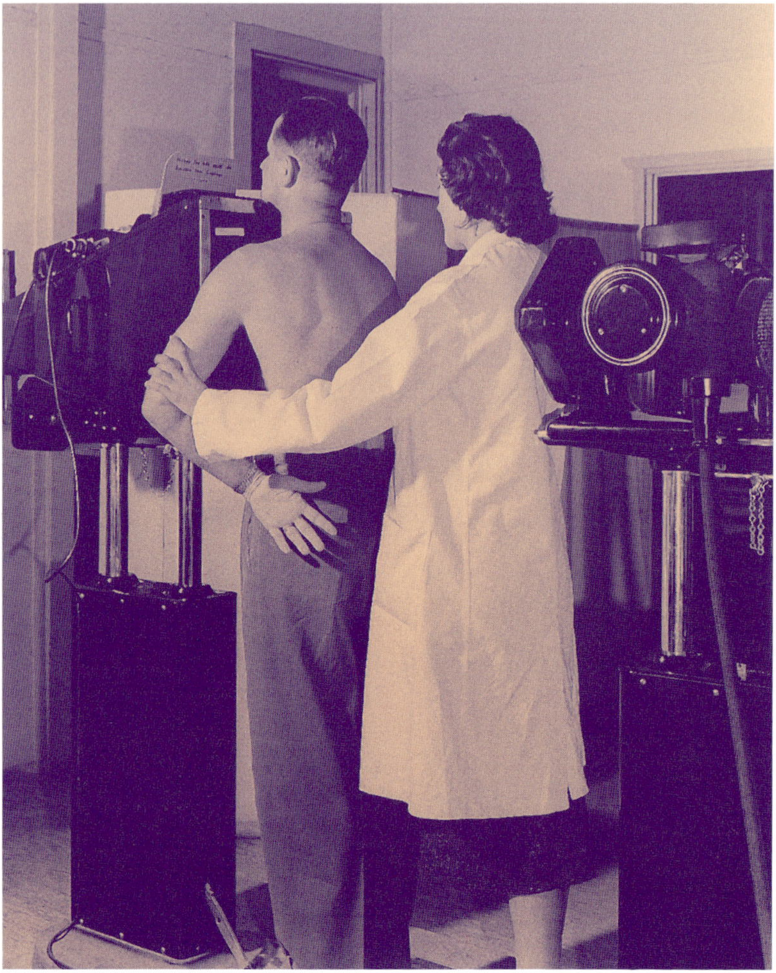

The SS Fairsea *sailed from Germany to Australia in July 1956. Passenger apprehension and boredom were alleviated by shipboard documentary films, health checks, and English lessons given by an Austrian teacher.*

The steps of uncertainty — both physical and mental: 'New Australians' disembarking from the Fairsea *at Sydney in 1957.*

The personal effects of the 100,000th European emigrant to Australia arrived, clearly marked, in Sydney in 1958.

Finding their new home on the world map. For refugee children, innocence was the key to hope as their parents struggled with dispossession and grief.

about seventy or eighty miles south of Darwin, where we camped among the bamboo. It was beautiful there.

The children thought it was Christmas every day. Barbara was not quite four, George was eight, and Stephen was close to twelve. It was a very happy situation because when I met Krys, the children and I sort of loved each other from day one. Because Krys had been a widow for a while they simply wanted a dad and right away they called me 'Daddy'. They had a great time on the trip. I knew something about football and the boys were crazy about football.

We then turned eastward towards Mount Isa, travelled almost to Cloncurry and came to a crossroads where one road went north and the other road went east. To decide which way to travel, we pulled out matches, broke one match in half — that was to go north — and left one match unbroken. I picked the short one, so we went north.

We travelled through Normanton, then a very tiny town, and arrived at Walker's Creek, which is halfway between Normanton and Karumba on the Gulf. It was a hot September day and the children wanted to go into the water, right at Walker's Creek. I had learnt to distrust tropical waters so I had a good look from the shallows and there were leeches everywhere. I showed the children and said, 'Look at that — a lot of bities.' And to top it all off, a ten-foot saltwater crocodile jumped from a bank into the water. I said, 'There's another bitie!' So we decided it wasn't all that hot after all and we travelled on to Karumba.

We pulled up at the base, which was unoccupied except for one fishermen. Krys asked him, 'Where's the shop?'

'What bloody shop?' he said.

There was no shop, nothing. But, there were wild ducks, fish, wild pigs, wild passionfruit — you name it. At first we camped at a disused fishing shack that belonged to a soft-drink manufacturer in Cloncurry and, from there, we established a temporary base — one mile further north at the end of the airstrip. Krys said, 'That will do me' and I said, 'Well, that will do me too.'

Krystyna In Karumba there weren't many people at all. There were two houses and an old chappy was living further out, near the boatshed. There was a little shack belonging to some people in Cloncurry, which they used when they came fishing. We asked if there was anywhere we could stop for a while and this old chappy said, 'Oh go and live in that shack — we know that those people won't come soon,' so we lived in that shack, which was good.

The children could play on the beach and catch fish. We liked it there, so we built a little house much further along the beach. It was nobody's land . . . well, not *nobody*'s — it belonged to *somebody*, supposedly. We lived there until 1959. The children had a great time. And then this old chappy offered to give to us one or two acres of land here — quite a bit of land then. So we went to the Shire Council and he said to them he wanted to give us the land. But they said, 'Well, you have to sell it.'

'No, I give it to her,' he explained.

'Well, you can't give it to her. You have to sell,' they stated firmly.

'All right — she can give me two pounds for it.' So we bought that piece of land for two pounds.

We liked it there, so we built a little house much further along the beach. It was nobody's land . . . well, not NOBODY'S – it belonged to SOMEBODY, supposedly.

Ron Once we were established, we wrote away to the Education Department. They leased to us a radio transceiver, which was all that was necessary to establish a radio station linked with the School of the Air on the Royal Flying Doctor Service radio frequency. The Queensland Primary Correspondence School had a course of study complementing the School of the Air program. We enrolled the children with both schools and their education was resumed. Moreover, the radio transmitter gave the children instant contact with teacher, doctor or police should an emergency arise.

We could leave the children on their own, and did so for anything up to a month. I taught both boys how to shoot because they would have to shoot to eat. Remember, there was no shop. Stephen had a shotgun and George had a rifle. I taught them that this was no toy; if they misused them, they'd go hungry or worse. Krys had taught Stephen how to bake bread — he was twelve or thirteen years old and he was a master baker by then. Everything fascinated them. George was an expert crabber and Barbara, well, she was Barbara — she kept us happy.

It was about this time — the end of 1955, early 56 — that we got our first crocodile. Barbara was playing on the beach at the water's edge with her back to the water and one day Steve came running up, 'Daddy, Daddy' — he couldn't speak, he was so worked up. He just pointed at Barbara.

There was a crocodile about fifty or sixty yards away. It was a ten footer and much too close to her back. Well, no problem, I shot him — and she never even heard the shot because there was a pounding surf and she couldn't have cared less. But we had to make sure that she wasn't upset. I left the rifle where I fired the shot and I went down and picked up Barbara to make sure she wouldn't see the dead crocodile and the blood in the water. She didn't, and I took her home and gave her a piece of cake and a cup of Milo. She loved it.

By the time I got back the crocodile was lying there and the tide had taken the blood away. What to do with it? We eventually consulted the old chap and he gave us a fair idea. It was the first skin we took and we got ten pounds for it, even though it was butchered up. That was about a week's wages! We figured this way: if we got ten pounds for a butchered skin, how much would we get for a properly taken off skin? We could see thousands of those ten-pound notes floating right around us, so that's how we developed an idea of how to hunt them. I built a boat and we set off hunting crocodiles.

We always began our night hunts with a bit of practice shooting. We had a large quantity of empty tobacco tins with us. They were only about an inch and a quarter thick and that is about the size of a crocodile's ear. Even though it was dark, Krys's shooting was good. She'd fire three or four shots, which meant three or four tins would sink after they were hit.

On an ordinary night, we would set out and Krys did the shooting while I was at the outboard. It took a lot of handling because if there is a five-knot current running, you have to steer the boat a little bit to the left of the target. At the same time, I was controlling the throttle. You can't change the speed of the engine abruptly as the crocodile will be frightened and submerge and that would be the last you'd see of him. So you had to work very carefully and at the same time hold the spotlight so it never left his eyes. If you missed his eyes — goodbye croc. The beam also had to go over the rear and front side of the rifle that Krys was holding, so it all took a fair bit of acrobatics.

We'd work all night and very often all of the following day because, after you finish shooting, you have to skin the crocodiles.

Then you'd eat — we ate mainly tinned food because there was no time for cooking. You had to work the tides and the tide waits for no one. Then we'd prepare for the next night, but if the tidal conditions were adverse, we didn't hunt and we'd switch to day hunting.

Krystyna When we went away the children stayed home and did their school work and they had to bake bread. They had to cook for themselves and even when the tourists used to come they used to say to Stephen, 'Bake us some bread because it's so lovely!'

So they'd look after themselves very well and sometimes, probably for a couple of days, they wouldn't do any school work and then they'd see our boat from far away and say, 'Oh, quickly!' and start doing their school work.

Ron I remember this one close call that I had. It was a dark night — as dark as you can get. No moon and the stars didn't do too much. I was out on the Norman River and in the distance, about three hundred yards away, we spotted the reflection of the eyes of a crocodile. So we went for it. At that time I used to catch live crocodiles for the Canadian market and if the crocodile was no bigger than about eight feet I would jump on top of him with a rope.

One end of the rope would be tied to the boat and I would jump on him and tie the other end of the rope around his lower jaw quickly. Then he'd bite the knotted rope and he'd stay put because a crocodile will never release what he catches.

Anyhow, this night we approached the crocodile, Krys was shining the spotlight and I could only see where the beam lit up. We eventually got very close to the crocodile and as I got ready to jump, I estimated that there would be no more than about three feet of water between the surface and the bottom and I thought the crocodile was about five feet.

After adjusting my bathers I jumped, but as I jumped, in that split second, I realised from the position of the head of the crocodile that the water was much deeper. In other words — the tide was much higher and the crocodile was about twice or three times the size that I would normally want to catch alive. I had my legs spread so I could get his head between my legs. As I jumped, he opened his jaws and snapped them shut about a quarter of an inch from my having a squeaky voice as a result of it. Well he escaped with my bathers — he bit them off. They were tight-fitting bathers, so I escaped with a fright, but Krys was laughing — it was a funny situation. It could have been *not* so funny, but we had had many close shaves and took such things for granted.

Krystyna At the end of the hunting of course we were very muddy so we'd go onto the bank and wash ourselves with a bucket — pour water all over ourselves and use our special soap for salty water. Then we'd go inside . . . heaven! A glass of wine, and we'd cook. Actually, I remember one time we were sick and tired of eating tins of corned beef, luncheon beef and things like that. So I said I would try to fry some crocodile meat from the tail. I did and Ron tried it and said, 'Oh, I'll have some more — it's lovely!' When we came back home and I told people that we tried crocodile meat, they said that we were cannibals. I don't know where they got 'cannibals' from but now people are buying crocodile meat.

It was dangerous, in a way, but no more than driving in traffic. Far more people get killed in traffic than among crocodiles.

Ron It was dangerous, in a way, but no more than driving in traffic. Far more people get killed in traffic than among crocodiles. And, of course, if you hunt them, then you have to approach them and you never know if there is another one just waiting for you. But then, if you know how to shoot fast, you live longer.

There was one incident that was not a particularly funny one and very close. I was in deep mud and I had to shoot from about a range of seventy yards because I couldn't get any closer to this sixteen-footer. I couldn't get a clear view of his head, so I had to estimate where his ear was because the earshot was the best way to kill instantly. But, not being able to see his ear, I just estimated — and of course I missed. I thought I'd killed him, but he was only knocked out. I wanted to reload the rifle quickly so that, on approaching him closely, I could shoot again but the rifle jammed and there was no way of getting it working.

I ran towards him and pulled out my heavy-calibre revolver. At about twelve inches (that's thirty centimetres) away, I fired a bullet into his head. I saw the base of the bullet flash with his bone and that was as far as it went. Very tough bones . . . I fired another shot and, well, eventually he had six bullets in his head and all that did was liven him up. Eventually he moved towards me, went right over me and then made straight for the water. I couldn't dodge him because I was knee deep in mud. He drove me into the mud like a tent peg. He just wanted to get into the water and I was in the way!

Krys heard all the shooting and thought another Korean War had started. As she zoomed towards me and I hollered over the din of the outboard motor, 'Throw me a rifle!' and she did. Then I sat down by the water's edge, but not too close, and waited for him with Krys's rifle. He came up and I don't think he really saw me. He was too sick. He just wanted to die on the bank. Well, he headed straight for me, so I just remained sitting until he was right in front of me, high and dry. I shot him in the head and that was it.

Commercial hunting is a terrible waste. I think that the average crocodile, speaking in terms of today's currency, was worth about $3000 to $4000 in meat and other products, but we were only taking a little bit of the skin and that was it. What we were doing made no sense.

Krystyna I remember one crocodile — we caught it on the hook. We were putting out baits and he swallowed it. We pulled the rope in and I remember he was a lovely, very light-looking crocodile. As I pulled him up he looked at me and seemed to say 'Why do you want to shoot me?' Really, he had such an expression in his eyes and face — 'Don't shoot me' — but he was on the hook and we *had* to shoot him.

Ron The novelty soon wore thin and in December 1965 I developed the idea of crocodile farming. From then on, we concentrated on developing a blueprint. There was no information on the subject, no literature on the saltwater crocodile as such, and I had to produce many papers, which were readily received by scientific institutions.

In January 1966 we flew to Brisbane for a discussion with the Queensland Premier, Sir Francis Nicklin, about our plan to establish crocodile farming in Queensland. We had known Sir Francis since the premiere, in Parliament House, of my first documentary television film about Krys, entitled *Woman's Strangest Job*. At the time, he and Speaker Sir David Nicholson insisted that that 'remarkable' movie be first screened before the Legislative Assembly in session, on 5 March 1964. 'The world must see that brave Queensland woman at her daily work,' they urged.

Sir Francis was sympathetic to our project and at once introduced us to Alexander Dewar, Minister for Industrial Development, and that department's head, Sir David Muir. Our local MP, Eddie Wallis-Smith, was with us at the meeting.

Our crocodile farming project was developing rapidly, considering our meagre resources, for the project was self-funded, and I now began a press campaign for the protection of the crocodile in the wild to enable a future industry initially to draw on the wild stock. We had great success and the media were behind us, as by then I was relatively well known. I had produced seven films and had published, worldwide, almost three hundred press and magazine articles on crocodiles, conservation and the Gulf of Carpentaria region of North Queensland. My contribution to the 1963 symposium, 'The World and Its People', in Rochester, New Jersey (US), and my exhibition at 1964/65 New York World Fair, had brought me unexpected acclaim.

Tragically, Sir Francis became ill and passed away. A new government was formed, headed by a man with views entirely opposite to those of the late Sir Francis. The new Queensland Government now stood firm; there would be no protection of the crocodile and no crocodile farming industry in Queensland.

Federal legislation allowed the export of wildlife and wildlife produce if it was taken in compliance with the laws of its state of origin. Western Australia and the Northern Territory had instituted some vague crocodile protection measures and now hunters continued to kill crocodiles there and brought the hides into Queensland where they were sold as being of Queensland origin. And everybody was happy with that. I fought a one-man battle, entirely without any support from any organisation or individual, which was later acknowledged by the Australian Museum.

By 1971 and 1972 I was being summoned to appear and give evidence before the House of Representatives Select Committee on Wildlife Conservation, where I had won great support for my cause.

To further discourage me from campaigning for the crocodile's protection and for the establishment of crocodile farming, the Queensland Government now took strong measures against me. By 1969 I realised that my only hope of success lay in taking my fight onto the platform of federal politics. The Australian press at once gave me generous support.

By 1971 and 1972 I was being summoned to appear and give evidence before the House of Representatives Select Committee on Wildlife Conservation, where I had won great support for my cause. Not one federal MP — Liberal, National or Labor — was against me. In November 1972 the Federal Attorney-General, Senator Lionel Murphy, announced what I had been pleading for: a total ban on all wildlife exports.

Over the many years my campaign was entirely self-funded, which proved a crippling drain on our resources, but Kris kept giving me the encouragement and support I needed when I was plain tired, and that almost alone gave the strength to fight on.

Perhaps the nicest recognition for my campaign and victory came from the United States. The University of Washington wrote to me about my being in the forefront of the new science of agriculture. America's politically most powerful wildlife and environmental protection organisation, the National Audubon Society, invited me to lecture across the United States and the Commonwealth of the Bahamas.

In the 1940s and 50s I often thought of Poland. No longer. Sixty years out of that country is a long time and I realised that you must never go back into the past because nothing will ever be the same. I would not live in Poland for $10,000 a day. I belong to the North of Australia

Throughout all those years in the Gulf we spent many a night at the campfire and discussed our lives — would we be wanting to do anything else — something else — whatever? Well, we were happy with what we were doing. We were happy with each other. We were perfectly happy . . . and that is as far as you can go in life.

In the 1940s and 50s I often thought of Poland. No longer. Sixty years out of that country is a long time and I realised that you must never go back into the past because nothing will ever be the same.

Journey of a Lifetime

The tale of Frank Buzolic

Frank (left) and his brother Nick

I come from the town of Hvar on the island of Hvar on the Yugoslav side of the Adriatic. My father was a labourer, a fisherman, a farmer, a jack-of-all-trades — he worked on anything and everything to make ends meet. In those days, there were no cars and we were able to play anywhere.

When I was about eleven years old, I was playing in a dinghy and I saw something silvery in the water. There was a spear in the boat, so I grabbed it and blindly thrust it down into the muddy water. When I lifted the spear up over the boat a big two-kilo cuttlefish fell off it. Now this was a miracle to me because there were never any fish in that enclosure — just tiny ones — and here I am catching a cuttlefish. I had never seen a cuttlefish bigger than about half a kilo.

At that very moment my mother was waiting in a queue to buy some fish at the fish market on the water's edge. Of course, I was so excited that I lifted the fish up in the air and said, 'Mum! Look! Mum!'

Everybody started saying, 'Do you want to sell it?'

But my mother said, 'Well, what do you think I'm standing here for?' I was a hero that day.

* * *

On 25 March 1941 the acting ruler of Yugoslavia, Prince Paul, bowed to pro-German support from the country's leaders and joined a pact known as the Rome–Berlin Axis. Prince Paul was one of the three regents who had been appointed to rule Yugoslavia after the 1934 assassination of the royal dictator King Alexander that saw Alexander's young son Peter II next in line for the throne. Two days after Yugoslavia joined the Axis, the military did away with the pro-fascist leaders and the seventeen-year-old Prince Peter was made King of Yugoslavia.

Hitler's reaction was swift and brutal, invading Yugoslavia on 6 April 1941. This was the beginning of the Nazi occupation and sowed the seeds for civil war.

Young King Peter escaped to London and appointed the army colonel Draza Mihailovich as the leader of the resistance movement, the Chetniks; on the other side were the partisans. At this stage both were still fighting the common enemy under the command of communist leader Josip Broz, better known as Tito.

As the end of the war approached, the struggle between the loyalists and the communists to gain control of the country intensified. Tito unanimously won power in the election of November 1945 and declared Yugoslavia a republic.

Frank Buzolic, his brother Nick and two friends Frano and Nikola escaped from a Yugoslavia in which one in every nine patriots had lost their lives during World War II. It was a country accused of acting as a western tool and blockaded by comrade Russia in 1948. And, to add insult to injury, it was a country forced to accept aid from the capitalist west because of a severe drought in 1950.

* * *

When the war started, it was very hard to get any food. People from the island went over to the mainland and bought any food they could. One boat that went over returned with bags of chestnuts — big 25-kilo bags. My father bought one of these bags of chestnuts and, boy, were they good! We boiled them, we roasted them, we even ate them raw, and we had them for breakfast, lunch and tea, until we had eaten all 25 kilos of chestnuts. By this time we all had bad breath and every time we belched it was really strong and tears would come to our eyes. So what does my father do? He goes and buys another 25 kilos worth of chestnuts! There was nothing else — you couldn't buy anything else. But we survived.

In the early part of the war, the Italians occupied most of Dalmatia and only a few Germans were there — just, I suppose, to keep an eye on things. But of course, in 1943, the Italians capitulated. They went on the side of America and England and so the Germans took them prisoners. At this time, my father started to do a little bit of black marketing. He would go to Dubrovnik and buy things and sell them in Hvar and in the villages. Then my father was caught up with the partisans so I started black marketing then, buying different things. I'll tell you the story about some cheese.

I knew that Germans didn't like the strong Parmesan cheese that they had taken from the Italians. The Germans were given hunks of cheese for lunch, and I used to go to the fence with a shoebox and I'd buy this cheese with a little bit of money. One particular German had a piece of cheese that was more than double the usual size, and he wanted more money. Well, I was quite cunning in those days — you had to be — and I just wouldn't give him any more money because I knew that he didn't like the cheese so he had to sell it.

I said, 'No! You've got the same piece as everybody else, so I'll give you the same money,' and I started walking away. He'd waited until last and I knew in my heart that he was going to call me back. He walked away and I kept walking away. The he said, 'Stop.'

I stopped and he said, 'All right — here.' I gave him the same money as everybody else.

Down the road, some people had been watching me to see what I was doing. They said, 'What were you doing up there?'

'I was buying some cheese,' I said. 'You wanna see it?' and I opened the box. They had a look and said, 'Do you want to sell some?' I just casually said, 'Oh, yeah . . .'

'How much?' they asked.

'Well,' I said, 'it all depends how big the piece is.' Now

this was a different kettle of fish, you see. The biggest piece was double the price of the smaller pieces.

Somebody bought it, and I had about two or three pieces left, which I sold then and there. I was selling them for about three times as much as I was buying them for. We were doing all that kind of thing. If you found out where you could get the stuff people couldn't buy, you could sell it anywhere. When you are a kid you're not scared of anything. You're not scared of dying, you're not scared of anybody — except if they want to belt you, and then you just run. That's it.

At one time, we were selling fruit to Italian prisoners. We were buying it at the market early in the morning, sometimes making two trips before the markets closed. The Italian prisoners had a little bit of money and of course they weren't fed too well, so you could sell them anything. One day, a friend of mine and I were going to sell them some fruit and up comes a German soldier. He had a couple of stripes and he let my friend go, so I thought, Oh well, he is not interested in us. But he must have seen that I was a bit scared because when I went past him he decided to stop me. He said, '*Halt!*' so I stopped.

'What have you got there?' he asked. I put down my box and showed him, thinking, He's going to buy it. He didn't even ask me how much. He just gave me one across the ear and said '*Raus!*' ('Get out!' or 'Get going!').

With the money I was making out of black marketing, I was buying food and fares for the tram and mainly keeping the family. I was thirteen when the Germans took over. I remember that you had to make sure you never spent more than you had earned; otherwise, next day you wouldn't have enough money to buy what you wanted to buy.

And it didn't matter what it was — shirts, trousers, shoes, fruit for prisoners, cheese (as I said) . . . anything you could find. I even found a place where I could buy boot polish. You couldn't buy boot polish in the shop and yet the factory was just up the road from me, so I used to go with a big tin and buy half a kilo or a kilo of boot polish, find a few empty tins that were discarded, fill them up, put a match to it and then blow the flame out and it looked just like factory made. We were selling it for three times as much and the people were still pleased to be able to buy it.

Now there was a factory that was making lollies — hard-boiled lollies. They were real hard ones. You couldn't buy lollies anywhere in the shop, but I could go over there and buy a kilo of lollies and put them in little bags and sell them at two hundred per cent.

At this time, I was thinking about going to join the partisans. My brother did and I asked him if I could come with him. He was only eighteen months older, but he was cleverer and he told me, 'No, you can't come with me. You are too young. They won't have you — they'll only send you back.' So I just stayed behind in Dubrovnik when the Germans occupied the city.

In 1944 in Dubrovnik there was never much food available. One day, I went and climbed this big mulberry tree right outside the wall of a sausage factory. I was minding my own business, just eating mulberries, when I saw this German soldier, who was apparently a worker at the sausage factory, shove something in his shirt and go outside the wall. I was as quiet as a mouse, watching him grab something out of his shirt and put it under a box just below the mulberry tree. He then walked inside.

As soon as he was inside the courtyard, I came down from the tree as fast as a monkey, put my hand under the box, grabbed it (whatever he had put there) and ran like mad. I ran for a couple of blocks before I turned around to see if anyone was following me. When I saw there was no one I opened it up.

I knew it was something big, some kind of meat. Anyway, it was a big thick salami! And straight away I cut some off and started eating it. When I got home I was a hero because we had some meat. Vegetables and fruit, you could get because the villagers were bringing them into the markets, but you couldn't get meat — and here was a dirty big salami waiting for me. I wonder what the German thought when he went to put his hand in and he couldn't find it! He probably wanted to take it to his girlfriend.

Well, after the war was over, I continued black marketing with my father and we had a little shop, selling salted sardines and fruit. Then, in 1947, there was a call for anybody who wanted to learn a trade in Czechoslovakia, so my father put me in for it. Out of about fifty kids, only two got selected and I was one of them.

My time in Czechoslovakia was quite enjoyable. The two of us learnt our trade in a small factory at first and then they put us in a big factory, where there were five hundred other apprentices. We were there for about eighteen months and I was learning to be a fitter and turner for that time. Then Yugoslavia split away from the Warsaw Pact and we had to leave within two or three days.

When we came back to Yugoslavia, they sent us to Rijeka. In Rijeka I worked in a torpedo factory for a couple of months. Later I moved into shipbuilding, which was next door. In the torpedo factory, we didn't have our own machines or anything so we just hung around. I attached myself to a tradesman and helped him. I was fortunate: every now and again he'd let me do a little bit and then a little more, until he found out how much I could do. I then passed my trade test and became a tradesman.

With communism, you work hard and you get nowhere. What kind of a life is that?

Even as a tradesman, life was very hard. You get the lowest pay as a tradesman when you first start. After you paid for your meals (we had a little cafeteria where we used to eat) and by the time you paid for your room, you hardly had any money to spend on yourself for clothing, entertainment or anything like that.

With communism, you work hard and you get nowhere. What kind of a life is that? You think about getting married, but how can you support a wife and children? So after about a year and a half my brother and I started talking about escaping. We thought we would like to go to America. First we thought about going over the border near Trieste, about escaping across the land, but if you got caught by the guards you could get shot. So you had to get a guide, but of course guides were pretty dear.

Just before we escaped I was called into the army. I wasn't quite *in* the army, but I went for the first interview. The first interview was the medical and after this, you were not allowed to leave town unless you told them your forwarding address. After the second interview you weren't allowed to leave town at all because within twenty days you would be recruited, so you had to stay at the address you had given them. If I left then I would be an army deserter and would have got ten years' jail. We decided to escape immediately by rowing to Italy.

It was 1950 and we took a ship from Rijeka, which is at the top of the Adriatic, south to Dubrovnik, which is near the bottom. As nobody had any money, my brother and I and two friends decided to steal a boat — a little dinghy, probably about a twelve footer — and a couple of sets of oars. The dinghy was anchored about twenty metres from the shore, so one of my friends got into the water and swam softly, without splashing, out to the dinghy, put the oars and his clothes in, and rowed around the headland to where we had walked and were waiting. He had to be careful he didn't splash too much while he was rowing: if you hit an oar flat on the water it makes a splash and the sound carries and can be heard far away. Across the water was Tito's villa and there was a guard patrolling the grounds.

It probably took our friend about an hour and a half to row to the spot where we were. When he turned up, it was half past midnight on, would you believe, Friday the thirteenth. I remember it well and so Friday is my lucky day. Anyway, we escaped like that and we rowed all night and decided to zigzag a little bit, go another way. Instead of going straight we went quite a few kilometres to the right and we could hear a launch that we thought was approximately where we were supposed to be. Later that night we got back on track, straight across the Adriatic.

We had put our measly gallon of water in the dinghy with a ham and a two-kilo loaf of bread. Believe it or not, we could not eat it because the ham was salty, the bread was dry and our mouths were so dry. We had finished our water in the first half day and had been drinking seawater — not very much of it, just a mouthful to moisten our mouths. It had a horrible, terrible taste. You'd want to spit out and your spit wouldn't go past your lips.

We kept on rowing. We were having a short swim every half hour to cool down in the middle of the day in the middle of the Adriatic. About the third day, after a swim, I grabbed the side of the dinghy and tried to get up. But I just let go and said, 'I can't make it.' At that moment, about a kilometre or more away, a swordfish jumped up in the air. I was in the dinghy before the swordfish hit the water again! So from then on I didn't complain about being tired.

My brother had been to nautical school to become a commercial navy captain and even though he was only there for a couple of years, he knew all the winds and weather and we had a compass. On about our second day, a gale blew up and the seas started to become mountainous. In between the waves, we couldn't see anything — that's how big the waves were. We were a bit scared, but my brother assured us that these winds would only last about ten minutes and then it would calm down. Of course it lasted ten minutes, just as he said.

We rowed for four days and on the fourth day, at 9am, we saw the coast of Italy. From the time we sighted the shores to the time we arrived there was another twenty-six hours — that's how far it was, or maybe that's how weak we were by then. We arrived next day, at 11am — exactly on the spot where we wanted to go.

Back at home, my father and my mother went to bed as normal. As youngsters, we went out with other young people, fooling around, maybe dancing. My parents did not know anything about our plans and when my father knocked at our bedroom door about 9 o'clock the next morning, saying, 'Come on you lazy bones — get out!' there was no answer. He assumed my brother and I had come home late and thought he'd leave us to sleep a little longer. So he yelled out again, at about 11am, 'Come on fellows, come on get out!' When no one answered, he opened the door — we found out about all this later on of course — and saw that nobody was there.

He walked to my friend Ivo's place and he asked, 'Are Nick and Frank here?'

My friend's father said, 'No, and Ivo is not here either.'

'Hmm, I wonder where they are. I wonder if they've had a fight and been put in jail.'

By that time it was 2 o'clock in the afternoon and my father went to the police to report us missing. Of course, the police knew straight away because somebody must have reported that their dinghy was missing. They put two and two together and then sent the launch after us. My father was interrogated in jail for a couple of days until they couldn't get anything out of him, as he knew nothing. It was years after, when he was sure that his mail wasn't being censored any more, that he told us in a letter what had happened and how he was locked up.

When we reached Italy, we were elated. We got out of the dinghy and the first thing we did was jump for joy and embrace each other. We thought, Freedom at last! We just danced on the shore. We felt like we were a little drunk because we had been in the dinghy and rocking for five days. When you get on shore, you've got to put your feet wide apart to make sure that you don't tumble over because you've got your sea legs and not your shore legs.

In Italy, freedom meant everything to us: freedom of speech, freedom of travel, freedom of work. In Yugoslavia, there was no freedom and because we were young people, we were kept under the thumb. I was asked to join the Communist Party in Yugoslavia and that was probably only a month or two before we escaped, so I was lucky. If you were asked to join the Communist Party, you didn't say no.

On the way to Italy we had decided to land not in a big city but in a smaller town where we could sell our dinghy and celebrate. But the Italian police wouldn't let us sell the dinghy without proof of ownership. They confiscated the dinghy and took us to the police station, where they started interviewing us. All we kept on saying was that we were hungry — can you give us some food? Anyway, we wore the sergeant down and he sent somebody to buy a loaf of bread and a few tomatoes and that was finished in no time at all.

After the interview we were left in the middle of the police station foyer and told to wait there. Across from us there was a prisoner in a cell, looking through the window. When he saw the guard had gone, he put his hand out and said, 'Come over, here.' I was bold enough to go over and he said, 'What did you do?'

I said, 'I killed a bloke.'

'Oh,' he said, 'you'll never get out of here.' And then he said, 'What about that other bloke over there?'

'That bloke killed two!' I said, pointing to my brother.

'Oh, you'll never get out of here.'

We were such cheeky possums — we gave cheek to anybody.

The jail beds were concrete, but on the first and second nights we had to hold on to the side because we still felt like we were rocking in the dinghy. It was only after the third night that we weren't too bad.

We didn't worry when the Italians put us in jail, as we knew that sooner or later we'd be free. I mean, we knew that when you go to jail you are only there until they prove you are not a criminal. After a few days, we were sick of jail so on the fifth day, when we put our dishes out through a little door at the bottom of the cell door, we decided that we were going to go on a hunger strike. But of course, when the food came, boy did we get stuck into it! There was no such thing as a strike.

From Italy we thought that Australia would probably be the best place to go. It was a new country — not like America, which was already an old, established country. Australia was full of opportunities and we had an uncle in

Australia, up at Innisfail. In Italy, when I was in a camp, people were talking about what is in Australia and the opportunities for being able to work and all that.

We went to a few different consulates: Canada was one and Australia was another one. We knew Canada was very cold and Australia wasn't that cold. Actually somebody told us that in Australia you go cane cutting up to your waist in water and I thought that was hard to believe.

On 1 April 1951 we landed in Melbourne. On the 2nd we started disembarking and got onto the buses. They took us to Bonegilla and we were there for about ten days — it could have been a fortnight; once you're free you don't count the days and hours. It was only a few more days before we got allocated jobs because at that time there were jobs everywhere. You leave one job, you can just turn around the corner and get another. I suppose we still weren't one hundred per cent free because we were under contract to work where they told us to work for two years. Not that I minded.

From there we went on the train through Sydney, stopping in Brisbane. Then we went to Calliope near Gladstone to work on the roads. We were digging ditches beside the road. Oh, it was hard in that sun!

We were extremely happy in Australia. We loved the new country. It was just what we thought it would be, but of

I had a suit that my uncle in America had sent to me in the camp, but that was all. One day I was playing sport in my suit pants and I went to pick up the ball and split a big hole in them.

course we had not known that the cities were as big as they were.

Australia was freedom — not only for us, but for all the migrants: English people, Italian people, for instance . . . When they come here they get a little bit disappointed, then they go back to their own country and they find out it is not as good as they thought it was and they come back again. So I never really worried about that because every place was a new place for us and we loved it.

The most important thing for my brother and me was to get jobs, food and good clothes. I mean, when we arrived in Australia I didn't have a pair of shoes. I had bought a beautiful pair of Italian shoes but I wore them out on the ship. The soles were actually made out of cardboard, but you couldn't see it because they were so well made. I had a suit that my uncle in America had sent to me in the camp, but that was all — I didn't have shorts or things like that. One day I was playing sport in my suit pants and I went to pick up the ball and split a big hole in them. Apparently it was a pretty old suit. So that is how much I had when I came to Australia.

After a couple of months in Calliope, they sent us to the bush to work, cutting lantana in between the young pine trees in the re-forested land. I didn't like the bush too much. I didn't like the snakes. So I ran away from there with my

One night, just before the dance finished, I took her to the tram and I asked her if she wanted to go out with me, but she wasn't quite sure. You know, new Australian, fast talker.

brother and caught the train back to Brisbane. Nobody asked me any questions. But of course I had to report to the Immigration Department. I just told them I'd got a job and that's all they worried about. After two years, they sent me a letter saying that I was allowed to stay in Australia indefinitely. So, after about five years, I got naturalised and at work they called me 'Aussie Frank'.

When my brother and I arrived in Brisbane we went looking for the dancing places. First we went to Italian clubs like St Francis' House, where they had dances on Sunday night, and then we discovered that there was a dance at Cloudland, which was a public dance hall. There was a cable tram going up to the top of the hill and there was this beautiful big dancing hall. Anyway, I saw this pretty woman so I thought, Oh, I'll ask her for a dance. I mean, she was the best-looking girl there as far as I was concerned. Although my English was pretty rough in those days, I could make myself understood. While I was dancing with her I asked her for the next dance; and while we danced the next dance, I asked for the next . . . In other words, nobody else could ask her because she was always dancing with me.

One night, just before the dance finished, I took her to the tram and I asked her if she wanted to go out with me, but she wasn't quite sure. You know, new Australian, fast talker. I said, 'Please yourself if you want to go out or not.' Then I said, 'Do you want to go to the pictures?' When I mentioned the pictures she thought, Oh, that'd be all right. So she said okay and we never looked back. I married her.

Australia has given me a very, very good life — from the very first day that I came here. When I started working, it just kept getting better and better. There's always 'downs', but mostly I've had 'ups'. I have absolutely no regrets. I'm so happy now, just thinking about the old days and how well everything worked out. We ended up having our own business and we raised eight children.

I'm extremely happy to be in Australia and to have had the life that we've had. We've always had plenty to eat and had good clothes. Comforts . . . we've always had comforts, from the very beginning, right up till now, and I can't see it changing, God willing.

We ended up having our own business and we raised eight children.

A Wog in the Soup

The tale of Beppi Polese, with Giuseppe De Carlo

Beppi

Giuseppe

For an Italian, lunch or dinner is not a daily necessity like filling the car with petrol; it's a refined pleasure. The table is a place where you talk, you enjoy and you celebrate. Food is an art form, an exchange of pure culture, a sign of acceptance. While breaking bread, fortunes are made, romance is born and friendships are forged in stone. To be invited to an Italian table is to be invited into an Italian heart.

The Romans in the Imperial Age are responsible for having turned cuisine into gracious bliss. For breakfast they excited the palate with grapes, olives and bread soaked in wine, leaving the climax for the evening banquet. Dinner was when the Romans truly feasted, with antipasto followed by game, pork, veal, goat, fowl, fish . . . and finally sweets with a honey base and fruit (fresh and dried). It goes without saying that no meal was complete without wine and song. This was the age in which the Italians lived to eat rather than ate to live.

It wasn't just the Roman Empire that conquered the world, but also the Italian cuisine — starting with Catherine di Medici when, in 1533, she went to France to marry King Henri II. Included in her dowry were her own chefs and pastrycooks. Between her and Marie di Medici — who did the same when, in 1600, she married Henri IV — they were jointly responsible for pulling France out of the culinary dark ages and instilling the basis for what was soon to be an eternally great French cuisine.

The Australian table in the 1950s was heavily influenced by the English, consisting of dishes such as steak and eggs, chicken Maryland, corned beef, roast lamb, roast beef and roast pork dressed with boiled vegetables. This was a cuisine that suited the English type of weather, but not Australia's semi-tropical climate. In this gastronomic void, a cuisine revolution was inevitable, with the arrival of the two culinary maestros, Beppi Polese and Giuseppe De Carlo.

* * *

Giuseppe When you talk about Beppi, you really talk about a legend, for the simple reason that Beppi is not just a pioneer in this business (with a lot of courage because he stuck with it while everyone else diversified badly); but Beppi *brought* food here, produced it, kept it, and improved it, and any chef in this state who has any name today has walked through Beppi's Restaurant.

Beppi That's right.

Giuseppe These days, they talk about pesto — Beppi used to make it in 1958!

Beppi Oh, yes. My father and mother-in-law used to grow the artichokes and herbs for me.

Giuseppe Mussels would never have come into vogue in Sydney if it weren't for you.

Beppi That's right. I used to get them myself at the Spit Bridge in Sydney when it was still a wooden bridge. Beppi's Restaurant was the first restaurant to serve mussels in Sydney.

Giuseppe And then they talk about, you know, the special mushrooms and the olive oils . . . you were playing around with such things when those people were still children.

Beppi Yes. When we arrived, it wasn't easy at all. I found it most difficult in 1956 when we opened.

Giuseppe We left Italy in 1950 because our home was bombed. We were homeless, and the International Refugee

We arrived here in April 1950 and they put us in a camp in Newcastle. My dad was a jeweller and they found him a job in a sawmill.

Organisation (the IRO) told my dad that, because we had become refugees, he had a choice: we could go to the United States of America or Australia. Dad chose America, but that had a twelve-month waiting time, while you could come to Australia within three months. So we came to Australia.

We arrived here in April 1950 and they put us in a camp called Greta, in Newcastle. My dad was a jeweller and they found him a job in a sawmill. The sawmill was in Brisbane, so we went to Brisbane around September 1950. He lasted something like two and a half years in that job before he cut off his hand, and that was the end of my father.

Beppi I came to Australia in the winter of 1952. The reason was that in Italy, in my profession, you could only find seasonal work, during the summer. But the summer work is not enough to sustain you throughout the year.

Giuseppe Brisbane in 1950 was completely countrified. I mean, people had two suits: brown with red stripes and blue with red stripes. A haircut was known as a 'pudding basin', with just a little tuft at the top of the head, and people thought we looked strange and funny.

Picture this: my mother arriving in Brisbane, going to the house, looking at the house, going to the shop, coming back crying. That's Brisbane in 1950. What can you get in Brisbane in 1950? Plenty of meat, plenty of fresh vegetables, plenty of butter, Coon cheese, cheddar cheese — that's it.

You wanted olive oil, you had to go to a chemist's shop. The chemist kept a few litres on his shelf for medicinal purposes. They didn't know what to do with olive oil.

Beppi Dripping.

Giuseppe Dripping, plenty of dripping. The great meal of Australia was roast mutton with potatoes and pumpkin. And if you wanted a coffee, for instance, it came out of a Bushell's bottle, chicory coffee bottle. That was coffee. If you dreamed about any type of cheese, forget it — it was a thing that didn't happen. If you wanted pasta, they wanted to know which tree it came from. People looked at spaghetti and they used to say, 'Oh, that's awful. We get better in tins.'

Or if you had a little bit of garlic, they used to turn their nose up at it.

But Australia was very rich in meat, fish, seafood, poultry, fruit and vegetables. It was very poor in the products we knew and had grown up with — products like coffee, cheeses, variety of flours. Pasta did not exist; spices, you couldn't find for love or money. You wanted olive oil, you had to go to a chemist's shop. The chemist kept a few litres on his shelf for medicinal purposes. They didn't know what to do with olive oil.

Beppi My first job in Sydney was at Romano's. It was a nightclub that had been established by an Italian who had come to Australia from England but was originally from

Italy, Mr Romano. The type of food that he had was more inclined towards the French cooking. But he also had chicken Maryland and steak and egg.

I worked six days a week, off on Sunday. And I was working actually about twelve to fourteen hours a day — lunch and dinner. I worked there for two years and then he sent me to work in his hotel in Wagga Wagga, where I managed the dining room.

Giuseppe In 1957 a guy opened up a place in Queen Street in Brisbane called the Milano Restaurant. And he got this Italian guy to make beautiful — really beautiful — gelato. He had an Italian cook and he was very good. It was a real Italian restaurant. The food was quite good but we couldn't *give* it away! I was so upset. One day, I went down to Queen Street and I had all samples of everything but ice creams. We wanted to give it to people, but we couldn't give it away!

Beppi At Romano's Hotel in Wagga Wagga I found something that was really very strange and demeaning. We had people coming in, even in the night time, in shorts and singlets. And these people, they were all farmers and sometimes they came in with boots full of mud, and I kept refusing them. One day the director of the hotel said to me, 'Beppi,' he said, 'you better stop doing that because otherwise we won't have any customers. These are our only customers.' I was so disenchanted that I left the job and came back to Sydney.

Giuseppe My dad wanted me to become a dental mechanic, which I hated. I tried it for two weeks, with people who stuck fingers in other people's mouths, and I really didn't like that. So they put me to work in an office and they were paying me four pounds, eight and six a week — nine dollars a week. That was around 1955 and I used to go and have a sandwich and a soft drink in this little place. This Sicilian guy, Rocco, was there, spending money like it was going out of fashion. So we became friends, and after about three or four weeks I asked him, 'What do you do that you can spend so much money?'

He said, 'I'm a waiter.'

I said, 'A waiter? How much do you make?'

'With tips, thirty-five quid a week.'

Thirty-five pounds — seventy dollars. I'm making nine, he's making seventy . . . What has this guy got that I haven't got?

So I went to the Carlton Hotel. It was supposed to have the best head waiter — Mr Cyril Smith was his name. He asked me what I wanted, and I said I would like to learn to be a waiter.

And he said, 'Why should I waste my time teaching you to be a waiter?'

I said, 'Look, I'll tell you what I'll do. I'll work for you for free for two months. If you think I'm capable of learning, you keep teaching me and you pay me whatever you want to pay me or you can tell me to go.'

I was there for six weeks and he put me on full wages.

Beppi I came back to Sydney in January 1956 and five, six months later I found that a restaurant called St James Restaurant, at the corner of Yurong and Stanley streets in Sydney, was for sale. So I came down and I looked at the place. It was a dining room with about ten tables and a kitchen and was very, very small. It was a Yugoslav place; they used to serve Yugoslav food. They had a type of food like . . . goulash. They had dumplings, big dumplings like tennis balls. And schnitzels . . . and all this type of food that was strange to me. But I decided to try my luck.

From a block away you could smell the mutton fat – a block away! And that was Sunday lunch, that was a special thing in Brisbane.

I remember the day that I took over — it was Sunday, 10 June 1956 — and I worked the whole day cutting tables down with a saw and readjusting chairs and so on, so we could open on the Monday. The Yugoslav owner used to serve food to the workers in this area and he used to sell food tickets in advance. For four and sixpence (forty-five cents), you got six meals for the week. I decided to carry on the same system that he had because I couldn't afford to change everything, yet.

It was around this time that I met my wife, Norma, and she was a great help to me. It would have been difficult without her love and support, particularly from the administration side.

Giuseppe I remember, this one time, mum went to a lot of trouble to invite six of our Australian neighbours home. She went to the chemist for oil and she scraped and crawled for some garlic and she waited for the tomatoes to ripen and she bought meats. Mum was a wonderful cook and she cooked a really wonderful three-course dinner. But the Australians wouldn't touch it! It smelled of garlic, the olive oil had an awful smell — they used to say if you ran over an Italian you could grease your car because of the olive oil.

Mum was shattered. But to add insult to injury these people invited us to their home for dinner two Sundays later. And from a block away you could smell the mutton fat

— a block away! And that was Sunday lunch, that was a special thing in Brisbane: roasted mutton with pumpkin and potatoes. And mum would not eat it. There was no way in the world that my mum would touch the stuff.

Beppi Part of the early success of Beppi's Restaurant was the kitchen exhaust fan. It used to blow the air outside onto the footpath. And, of course, the air used to carry the aroma of what we were cooking all the way up to William Street. A lot of people used to come in and say, 'We had to find out where this lovely aroma comes from . . . where all the flavour is. It smells magnificent.'

And I built up the business slowly like that also — by the smell of the nose, you might say.

Giuseppe In 1958 we had a house in Breakfast Creek in Brisbane and one time, when the fishermen came along, mum went up to them and asked if they ever had any calamari.

They said, 'Oh yes, we get them, but we use them as fish bait.'

And she said, 'Could you bring me some the next time you come in?'

The next time they came in, they brought her a wheelbarrow full of the damn things. So mum, out of the goodness of her heart, asked them to have a cup of coffee and sit down. Of course they hated the coffee: it was too strong, too black and all this other garbage — they just wanted dirty dishwater with a bit of sugar, that's what they were used to as coffee. But mum actually cooked some calamari for them. Now, out of eight fishermen, four of them went berserk on it and four of them didn't like the taste of the olive oil and that was the end of it. Every week we had a wheelbarrow full of calamari.

But if you tried to buy them, you couldn't. You could

When we came over here, we could buy a gallon of red wine in a bottle for two and sixpence (that's eighteen litres for a dollar), and it was excellent wine.

buy lobster at seven shillings a pound — a dollar forty a kilo. You could buy prawns for a dollar a kilo. But you couldn't buy calamari. And anyway, if you can buy lobster at a dollar forty a kilo, why would you want to eat calamari? That was the logic of it. This is why Beppi was so great and so courageous. Mussels . . . who the hell would want to eat mussels when you can get oysters for the equivalent? Because for oysters in those days we used to pay six shillings a dozen, you know. Now why would you want to eat mussels? But Beppi had the persistence and he had the knowledge, so he always had the edge.

Beppi You know why this happened? I'll tell you why: because I learned. I learned in the old times. I learned because I started as an apprentice. I was serving the floors. I used to bottle the wine with the owner in the cellar in Milan. I come up from the bottom, the very bottom. I was working seven days a week.

Also I learned for the reason that, in Italy, as I said, we never could find work in the winter because there are very few winter resorts so I had to go and work in different cities. Working in different cities, I picked up so much knowledge, so many different ways of cooking, so much knowledge of things that it helped me to become what I am today.

Giuseppe But let me tell you about great things in Australia

The white wine, it was okay: it was accepted as wine. But the red wine, people used to put sugar in it, because they thought it was coffee.

which we can't forget. When my dad came here in 1950 he used to drink his wine because that's what we drank in Italy. And when we came over here, we could buy a gallon of red wine in a bottle for two and sixpence (that's eighteen litres for a dollar), and it was excellent wine.

As a matter of fact, if Beppi remembers properly, he can remember that in the early 1960s he could buy a bottle of Grange Hermitage for around five shillings (fifty cents). Which was wonderful! You could get terrific red wines, but no whites.

Beppi When we first opened Beppi's Restaurant the liquor laws were very different from today. To get a liquor licence was very, very difficult. You had to apply to the licensing board of course, but also you had to have a permit from the owner of the building. In our case the owner was a tee-totaller and he refused to give it to us because he didn't believe in alcohol. This for me was a problem: I had a restaurant but I couldn't serve alcohol. So what I used to do was to serve the wine with the food without asking them do you want wine or not. And not to make it too obvious, I used to serve it in teacups. The white wine, it was okay; it was accepted as wine. But the red wine, people used to put sugar in it, because they thought it was coffee. I carried on like that until I finally got a liquor licence.

Giuseppe A good coffee in this country came around about 1960/61, when Luigi Coluzzi opened the Coluzzi Bar in William Street. That was the only coffee in the state of New South Wales. The Coluzzi Bar was an instant success with Italians. The Italians were there from 8.30 in the morning until midnight. It became the meeting place.

Good coffee was only at the Coluzzi Bar . . . until about 1985. Coluzzi always used very ordinary coffee and he made fantastic coffee. Thank God for Coluzzi.

Beppi In the 1950s we also encountered a lot of difficulty from the health inspectors. They used to come into the kitchen and see the pots and see the things that we used to cook, and they used to question what we were doing. They would see the stockpots and say, 'I think this dish here is a bit off.'

And we explained that the stocks are cooked today for tomorrow, to have the right consistency and combinations of flavour.

Or they would ask, 'What's this?' We'd say, 'Chicken.' And they'd say, 'No, I think this is rabbit.' And of course we would show them the raw material and convince them. When they learned what we were doing they actually left us alone.

I also had a few arguments with customers who would say, 'No, this isn't chicken. It's rabbit.' And I used to tell them, 'Look, the chicken is much cheaper than rabbit. If I serve you rabbit, then the price of the dish will be twice as much as this one.'

Giuseppe What also was very good in the 1950s and early 60s were the hamburgers. The hamburgers cost about twelve cents each, but you used to get a big hamburger, beautifully cooked, with grilled tomatoes and grilled onions in a heavy bun with lettuce and tomatoes and *a piece of beetroot* — and tomato sauce with chillies in it. And the hamburgers were really beautiful because they were just grilled and they were really good and they were always done by Greeks.

Milkshakes were another wonderful thing. They used to cost you three cents. You used to get a big milkshake with milk, a large scoop of ice cream, beautiful chocolate or vanilla or banana or whatever you wanted — malt was extra. And they were really beautiful.

Those things were really good.

Beppi You couldn't find artichokes at the time. You couldn't find a lot of things that in Italian cooking you require — like basil, for instance, and other spices. So my father and mother-in-law, who were retired, used to grow these things for me, the artichokes and everything. Also, they had friends and their friends used to grow the necessary spices and ingredients that I used in the cooking. And I remember my wife Norma saying to me, 'No, don't make them work. Leave them alone.'

'No,' I said, 'They need to do something. They need to be needed.' And we created an atmosphere that was very good — a family atmosphere.

Giuseppe In 1957 the first Italian delicatessen opened in Brisbane — Finucan opened the first delicatessen. He brought olives and cheeses and salami and prosciutto and olive oils of all types, tins of tomatoes . . . And that's where we went berserk — the Italians went berserk — and this guy made an instant fortune. Anyway, there was something like 300,000 Italians in Brisbane, and this guy opened the one and only store. I mean, he just used to bring the products in by the boatload and he'd get through them in no time at all. He thought he was in heaven!

And we thought we were so lucky to get those things there at that particular time.

Beppi The 1950s were an education for our customers and for us. I remember when I started to use and serve pheasant. The way you prepare the pheasant is you hang it by the neck for two or three days with the feathers until the meat gets tender.

It happened once that the customer called waiter and said, 'I don't know. I think there is something wrong with this dish.'

I went over myself and I said, 'Sir, this is pheasant. Did you ever have pheasant before?' He said 'No' and I explained, 'Well, this is how the pheasant is supposed to be cooked and how it is supposed to taste.'

He said, 'Look, I'll have the pheasant, but I want you to have the first bite.' So I tasted it and said it was good and he was happy.

But after that, instead of hanging the pheasant for two days, I'd only hang it overnight. And I overcame the problem because it wasn't smelling as strong as it was supposed to be.

Giuseppe Things we take for granted today just weren't eaten. It's not that they weren't here; they just weren't seen as food. For instance, offal — liver, kidneys, heart and things like that — they used to give them to you for free. You used to go to the butcher and say, 'Can I have a liver?' They would give it to you for free, anytime you wanted it and as much as you wanted, because they had no use for it.

Tripe . . . I mean tripe was never used. Beppi's is the only restaurant in Australia that I know of that made tripe

'God,' they used to say, 'we use these things as a bait to go fishing!

continuously because he had a certain following of people that ate tripe. They used to give prisoners in jails tripe. You could ask the butcher and he'd throw you as much tripe as you wanted, for nothing.

Kidney used to go with the chops, so they used to leave them with the chops and people used to throw them away. The only thing that cost a small amount was brains.

Beppi I used to go with Norma to the Spit Bridge, often at four in the morning when the tide was low so I could pick these beautiful mussels under the low water mark. To introduce them to people, I used to serve them and give them away for nothing . . . and still I had to convince them to try.

They used to ask me, 'What is it?'

'God,' they used to say, 'we use these things as a bait to go fishing !' And I used to tell them, 'Well, if the fish like them they must be good!'

And I used to say, 'Try and I'll tell you after. If you like it, I'll tell you. I want you to try it first because if I tell you, you won't have it — doesn't matter how good it tastes.' So they used to try them and like them and then I used to tell them: 'These are mussels, this is octopus, this is calamari . . .'

And I used to tell them, 'Well, if the fish like them they must be good!'

But I made adjustments to the dishes according to the need . . . the flavour, and taste of the customers.

Giuseppe Did you sway a little bit toward the Australian way to satisfy also the people who did not like the Italian food?

Beppi Not really, I didn't . . . I never lost my Italian base, identity. I changed the flavour. Because I used to talk to people, listen to them. And for instance where you use bay leaves or sage, I used to use rosemary. And vice versa. But I never lost the basic identity of Italian cooking.

Giuseppe I must confess, I did. I did change to please the non-Italian palate. But what happened in 1975, actually, was that the Italian kitchen just took off madly and you could be more traditional Italian and that was terrific.

Beppi The food ignorance that was here in the 1950s wasn't even their fault; a lot of Australians didn't travel very much because it was such a big distance between Australia and Europe, so they didn't know. There were some people who knew because of the experience they had during the war — being in the army, being stationed in Italy — but that's it.

What's important is that we have come a long way in fifty years.

Giuseppe The 1950s were wonderful years, and they were an excellent opportunity for the cuisine in this country to flower, to bloom . . . And every single Italian restaurant owned by Italians, in their own way, has helped because if they were bad or good it makes no difference; the fact is that they were there and they were trying. Now, if you really talk about food — Which is the most popular food? No, which is the most *sold* food? — it has to be the Asian food. But which is the most *liked* food? It still is Italian food.

Beppi We've come a long way and we still have a long way to go, but with the fantastic products that we are getting today, the availability of those products commercially, the future in the restaurant business will be extremely exciting.

Beppi Giuseppe

Which is the most popular food? . . .
It still is Italian food.

Dutiful Daughter

The tale of Hideko Coombes

World War II brought a proud Japan to its knees. Nearly all major cities, except for Kyoto, were practically levelled by wave after wave of air attacks.

It took the first two atomic bombs ever to be used in warfare to bring about the unconditional defeat of Japan and on 2 September 1945 Japan surrendered. The war cost Japan 2,144,507 lives and a staggering A$100 million in reparations claimed by the Allies.

Within two weeks of surrendering, Japan was placed under the control of the Allied occupation forces, with General Douglas MacArthur as supreme commander. Australian soldiers played a part in the occupational forces.

During the occupation hundreds of Australian soldiers fell in love with Japanese girls but the white Australia policy still guarded our shores. It was not until 1952, with a change in the law that they were allowed to marry. Some 600 Japanese women then migrated.

Hideko Coombes was one of them. She was a respectable young Japanese girl looking for work with the Allied occupation forces. Her fiance was an Australian employment officer. From a chance meeting grew a love story between two opposing cultures that was to last a lifetime.

* * *

To be a Japanese dutiful daughter meant you were expected to obey the parents, particularly father, who was the head of the family. But I was a real tomboy. I liked to climb trees, I wanted to jump over little streams and whatever the boys did I wanted to do the same. As far as I was concerned, it was a mistake that I came to this world as a girl. But, of course, in Japan everything was segregated. Girls were supposed to be gentle and we were not allowed to copy what the boys did. So there was a very strict line between boys' lives and girls' lives. And we had to obey that. If we broke that code of behaviour, we were chastised very severely.

My father was very strict. I am one of four sisters — no brother. In fact, before I was a born, there was a boy but he died very young. My father never forgot about that and he always considered it to be his misfortune because that meant that there was no one who could continue our family name. And of course in Japan in those days, and even to a certain extent now, boys are supposed to be more important.

My father was a typical, respectable Japanese man. He was interested in Japanese martial arts, Japanese arts and Japanese music; there was no trace of western culture in our family. I was born and brought up in a place called Kure, in the Hiroshima area. Kure had one of the biggest naval operations in Japan. And my father's business was to tailor-make uniforms and also civilian clothes for Japanese naval officers — and no one but officers. This contributed a lot to his feudalistic way of thinking.

My mother was a very gentle, typical Japanese woman who worked very hard. I think in lots of ways my mother worked much harder than my father. As a merchant wife she played a great part in the business itself but she never came to the surface. It was expected for her to serve my father and that was it. This was the same in every household.

As far back as I can remember my mother worked, worked, worked — all the time. And she never complained. She never answered my father back. In lots of ways my father was, well, you might say a tyrant. But I know he was a good man. He was very responsible and he worked very hard. In fact it is hard to remember if they ever sat down and enjoyed their leisure. When did my mother sit down and enjoy a cup of tea? Or read a book? I can't remember, I really can't remember. And now, when I look back, it's amazing my mother lived to the ripe old age of over eighty years. So in a way maybe hard work doesn't hurt us so much.

Even at school there was a difference between boys and girls and everything was segregated too. Boys and girls did not sit in the same classroom — they were separated. Later on, in high school, boys studied different subjects, such as a much higher level of mathematics and science, and girls were not allowed to study these subjects. Instead we had to study home science, sewing — things like that. There was a very strict rule at school and at home that we were not to mix with the opposite sex. For instance, even when you were walking around the street and you saw your own brother, you weren't allowed to talk to him.

In high school, if you were caught talking to the boys on the street, you might have been suspended from school. Or, in worse cases, you might have been expelled. And that was the life of ordinary Japanese people before War World II.

As far as I can remember, Japan was very aware of western powers invading or seeping into Asia and colonising countries. It was not just the British but also the Spanish, the Dutch — even Germany was coming into Asia. There was also Russia from the north. The Japanese were quite worried that Japan was going to be colonised too. So the government and the military were very busy using propaganda to paint an evil picture of western powers. They were very busy indoctrinating the Japanese people into believing that we had to have a strong military power to protect ourselves.

English language used to be one of the compulsory subjects, but I can remember in the second year of my high school life it was suddenly stopped. Nobody was allowed to study English because that was evil countries' language.

The propaganda war was very fierce. We were prepared to endure any hardship in order to protect our country. So, as far as I can remember, starting from primary school, this was always part of our education.

At about the time when I went to high school Japan got

involved in the war with America. And it was around that time we started to experience hardship: things became quite scarce and everything was rationed. We were told we had to endure hardship in order to win the war.

We were told to do everything not to be captured, even at the very worst time — that is, if Japan was invaded. We were told to commit suicide rather than be captured. And towards the end of the war when things were really bad, with lots of cities bombed, we were told that if we came face to face with enemies we were to get a bamboo stick and cut the top very sharply and to use it as a spear. Everyone knew this was quite ridiculous but we had no freedom of speech, so nobody spoke up. We just swallowed that sort of instruction. But gradually things became so much harder.

The war time is something that people of my age will never be able to forget. We used to think that Hiroshima would be bombed before Kure, but we were wrong. Kure was first. About a month before the end of the war, the Kure residential area was bombed and we lost our house. Japanese houses are built mainly out of timber and paper. So, it didn't take much time to burn the whole thing up.

I remember, one night when we had air raids, people told us — my mother and my second sister and myself, who were the only ones at home — to get away from there: it was too dangerous. So we did and we ran towards the park. On the way a fire bomb was dropped right on top of our heads. I realised my clothes were on fire, as were my mother's, so we jumped into a big water tank. But that wasn't very safe either, because the fire was floating on top of the water tank. So we had to jump out. I noticed that my sister, who didn't jump into the water tank, was jumping around, avoiding the fire on the road. And we eventually got to the park and then to the river. There were lots of big

This cloud was growing, bigger and bigger – right on top of our heads. And it stayed there for quite a few days.

rocks in the river, so we got into the cavity of a big rock and covered ourselves with a blanket that we had brought with us. I was not all that scared at that time but afterwards I had terrible delayed shock.

Overnight we lost everything, including my father's business. That was a very sad night.

One morning, about three weeks after Kure was bombed, we were in the country doing our washing and we saw this terrific flash of light. It was as blue as you could imagine and very, very strong. The light was much bigger than the biggest lightning I had ever seen. Then quite a few minutes later — I can't recall how long it was, but quite a few minutes later — we heard this great big sound, like a huge bomb or something exploding.

We were in the bush, so we didn't have anyone else to talk to at the time. Later on, when we went down to the old area of Kure, the whole place was talking about this terrific flash and the terrible sound but nobody knew what it was. Then suddenly we discovered over our head a huge cloud. And this cloud, too, was like nothing we had ever seen in the past.This cloud was growing, bigger and bigger — right on top of our heads. And it stayed there for quite a few days.

People started to talk about this flash and huge sound of explosion as *pickerdong (picker*, that's the word for flash; and *dong*, that means explosion). That was the onomatopoeia name of what we later found out to be the atomic bomb.

Atomic bomb? Nobody had ever heard of that. And this atomic bomb was told to us by the radio and the newspaper quite a few days later. Nobody knew what it was.

In actual fact quite a few men went to help the people of Hiroshima from Kure and I saw some men who had just come back from Hiroshima. We wanted to find out what had happened to Hiroshima. We asked but nobody told us. Later I realised it was such terrible scenes that they saw and experienced, such horrific things that nobody wanted to talk. They just said, 'No, you women and children do not have to find out.' So those people who saw terrible things never told us anything. And quite a few years later — after I came to Australia — I read a novel called *Black Rain* and I was absolutely shocked!

I was shocked about my ignorance. I lived not far from Hiroshima and I went to have tertiary education there but I still did not know the details of what happened to each individual.

Soon after Hiroshima, Nagasaki was bombed by another type of atomic bomb and by then the Japanese people started to feel quite desperate. I think Japanese people's general ideas were that we were far from winning the war. And it was quite clear that the military was prepared to sacrifice everything. They were prepared to lose so many people's lives but they were not prepared to think about the end of the war until we won.

The atomic bomb was the deciding factor and who stopped the fighting was the Emperor. The Emperor was supposed to be god. We were not allowed to hear his voice or look at him for any reason because he was such a remote person to us. He made a very important speech on the radio.

It was the first time we heard the Emperor's voice and he told all Japanese that this was the end of the war. We must stop fighting and we must start building Japan in a very peaceful world. If he did not talk to us on the radio, many people would have committed suicide. I was working in a factory when I heard the Emperor's speech and my first thought was, I hope my father didn't commit suicide.

After the war Japan started to change — very, very rapidly. To start with, the American occupation forces came in. And suddenly Douglas MacArthur was the Supreme Commander and he was the person who governed Japan for quite a few years.

What was very important was that without Japanese people fighting, we were given democracy. In lots of ways I think that probably built the foundation of the new Japan. And also, we women were given equality! That was big news for me. So Japan rapidly started to change. Of course, we had to endure quite a few years of scarcity of creature comforts.

Japanese people started to have some ray of hope for the future. And the language that we had not been allowed to study became a very strong power because the main industry and main jobs were with the occupation forces. The people who had prior knowledge of English were in the driver's seat. And now the Americans and British who were seen as closer to devils than people before the war were now being seen as human beings.

Before the occupation forces came in we were told that they were going to do terrible things to us. So women and children were evacuated to the country area. I went to live at my grandmother's place in the very remote country area. But soon we discovered that, no, nothing terrible was happening in the city, so we gradually came back and started to study English madly.

After the war I went to study English at the university in Hiroshima. When I graduated, naturally, I wanted to seek a job using my skills in English. So I went to have a job interview at the British Commonwealth Forces. The employment officer was an Australian sergeant. I was prepared to use my English, however poor it was, but I couldn't believe my ears when I heard Japanese spoken by this Australian sergeant. I got such a shock. I thought, Just a minute; his Japanese is much better than my English. I was so shocked and quite intimidated and I thought to myself well wherever did he learn Japanese? Despite my poor English I did get the job and I started to work doing very simple translations and this and that.

One day after work I was going to meet up with my oldest school friend but it started to rain and I didn't know what to do. I was just waiting outside my workplace, hoping that the rain would stop, when along came this Australian sergeant. He offered me a lift and then waited for a while and took us home.

That was my first personal encounter with my future husband and after that time we started to meet up after work. He was a very happy-go-lucky, easygoing person with a sense of humour. He used to make my family laugh a lot.

Slowly we got to know each other and — surprisingly, when I look back — my husband was the first person who treated me as his equal, not as a man from the country that conquered us. Also he kept telling me: 'Don't denigrate yourself because your country lost the war. You are building up your country and you have your equality with men. too. You just have to change your way of thought. You have to assert yourself.' Well, that was something I liked to hear very, very much!

He taught me how to think as an individual and surprisingly we had a lot of mutual interests in art, literature and music. Although he did not have a formal education he was much better educated than myself in every way. In Japan we have a bad habit of thinking that formal education is the only education. That is not true. You didn't have to go to university to educate yourself. You could self-educate yourself.

Gradually my way of thinking changed a lot. Before that, well, I just had to digest what they told me and I just had to follow the system, so to speak. I suppose I was strongly drawn to him and his way of thought.

Now, my father had his traditional ideas of whom I had to marry. Of course Japanese marriage is not for each individual but it is primarily for the family, and your individual happiness comes second place. My father naturally wanted me to marry a respectable Japanese man with a background similar to my respectable family. An Australian soldier did not come into his thought at all.

But as this man and I got to know each other more and more, we started to think about marriage. I explained to my future husband that my idea was very untraditional and naturally I was going to hurt my father's feelings very much. So I wanted to follow Japanese tradition as much as possible, in order to keep my father's dignity and also soften the strong objection I was expecting. So we had to do the right thing.

According to the tradition we decided to use a go-between: *nakudo*, in Japanese. I thought, since my father respects officers so much, we should use an Australian major who spoke fluent Japanese. Instead of having just one go-between my future husband also thought of using a Japanese person who thoroughly understood the Japanese tradition.

They went to put the marriage proposal to my father. My father was very diplomatic at the time. He did not raise any objection, he did not raise his voice very much, and in fact he was very calm. His answer was that he would think about it. So those people all thought the meeting went very well, that they had succeeded. But it was not so at all. My father had not changed his mind. He thought the proposition was absolutely outrageous. He had to squash this down, no matter what. From the next day I was detained at home; I was not even allowed to go to work. He wanted me to cut my relationship with my future husband completely. But we were much more cunning than that.

Meanwhile my husband went to make arrangements for the marriage, in the form of registration at the Kure City Hall. He made an appointment.

As I was detained at home I pretended that I had to contact my office in English, but I was ringing my future husband and I found out when the date was. On the day I was to get my belongings together and come out. I still thought that day I could come home but my future husband and his friends said once you went home that would really be the end of it.

After the marriage, my husband told me to ring my father and tell him about it. My father said, 'All right, come home. It doesn't matter, just come home.' I couldn't take the risk. After that we went to Kobe where the British Consulate was and for the Australian side we got married there again — another registered marriage. Then, about a month later, I had a church wedding. So I had three weddings.

But mind you, I still had a great sense of guilt. I was still not doing the right thing. I was not behaving like a dutiful daughter, according to Japanese tradition. And that used to worry me a great deal. Of course, the problem was that it was a marriage of two different cultures.

Australia had the White Australia Policy. So they still did not, actually, recognise coloured people to come to Australia. That was a huge stumbling block. Americans accepted the Japanese to go to America but the British had to change their rules a little in order to allow Japanese brides to come to Australia on humanitarian grounds.

Before coming to Australia I knew very little of this country. We learnt a little in Geography, but only a tiny bit: Bondi Beach and the Harbour Bridge. After I was married and before I came to Australia, we attended some courses sponsored, I think, by the YWCA and we had a lecture on our legal rights and how to become a good Australian housewife. We were taught some cooking. I learnt how to cook roast leg of lamb. Altogether, at that time, about three hundred Japanese brides came to Australia.

I asked my husband if he could possibly make his life in Japan, but he thought it was very difficult indeed. What was he going to do in Japan? And besides, I think he really wanted to come back to Australia. I was still old fashioned in lots of ways and I thought, Well, I have to follow my husband. In the corner of my mind I felt, of course, Australia might give me a completely new life. So there was a bit of a sense of adventure for me, too. Although leaving Japan meant that I might not be able to see Japan again . . . but that was a chance I had to take.

At first, when my husband informed his father that he had married a Japanese woman and he was going to bring his Japanese wife to Australia, my father-in-law was not pleased at all. So my future husband suggested that I write to him myself.

I started to write him, talking about my family. Well, it was very important that he knew I was from a very respectable family and that I wasn't a gold digger or harlot, and I explained my education and interests. After about the third letter, he seemed to have changed his mind, and his attitude had changed. And when I came to Australia he helped me build my new life.

Well, the day I left Japan, I left Kure by train, with the whole family, except my second sister who was living in a different part of Japan, there to send me off. And that day my father told me that if my marriage did not work out I could go back to Japan. Well, I thought that that was the word of acceptance from my father. But I thought, If my marriage breaks up, how could I dare go back to Japan? So I had to make my marriage successful, no matter what.

The Australian Army got us an opportunity to travel from Japan to Australia by a tourist ship that was making a round trip from Australia to Japan via Hong Kong and Cairns. Although I was lucky enough to travel with my husband, we were not allowed to share a cabin. That was too luxurious, that was too much like a holiday. So that's how we came to Australia.

On 23 September 1953 I arrived in Australia. I thought Sydney was beautiful: Sydney Harbour, the Botanic Gardens and then behind the Botanic Gardens there were beautiful statuesque buildings. I thought that they looked very dignified. But very quiet. Very quiet place. There weren't many people around.

Our ship was berthed at Woolloomooloo, and after a while my husband spotted his family waiting near the Botanic Gardens. I was quite moved. I knew they came to see my husband but I was with him too and I thought if they did not approve of my husband bringing a Japanese wife they did not have to be there. So I was very pleased.

After I got off the ship I was driven to my parents-in-law's house in Lane Cove and the first thing I noticed was that there weren't many people on the street. Was it a public holiday or something? The quietness of the place was quite striking compared to overcrowded Japan.

It was springtime in Sydney and each house had a red roof and a front garden and flowers. Everything looked so different from Japan, but so beautiful. These days Australian people often talk about uninteresting brick buildings and red roofs, but to me everything was so dignified and so beautiful compared to the rather flimsy Japanese buildings. You must remember Japan was devastated by the war.

I found out, twenty-five years later, when my husband's sister-in-law told me, the first impressions they had of me and about the whole family's attitude towards me. You see I'm very small — not even 150 centimetres tall. And I was twenty-four years old when I arrived but the first time they saw me they thought I was about fourteen or fifteen — a little girl. My husband's family is made up of big people: my eldest brother-in-law was about 196 centimetres tall and everybody was so much taller, with a much bigger build. I was even much smaller than my husband's thirteen-year-old niece. So they had to change their preconception about me straight away and they became very protective.

My father-in-law, in lots of ways, didn't know how to take me, I suppose. In the 1950s there were so many people who were very anti-Japanese and they did not like Japanese war brides coming to Australia. But we wouldn't go to the pub to drink, so apparently quite a few older friends of my husband and even the neighbours chastised my husband for bringing home a Japanese wife. And who was the one to stand up and defend my husband? My father-in-law.

In Australia my husband gave me a lot of freedom to do what I wanted to do and when I first arrived here I was living with my in-laws. In Australia, the concept is to have no more than one woman in the kitchen, so I did not have enough to do at home. I decided I should maybe get a job and go to work. But what job? How to get a job?

Well, that was a big trouble and then the wife of one of my husband's friend's very kindly offered to take me out for a job interview. She took me to a department store called Anthony Hordern's and to my surprise I got the job that day as a clerk in the correspondence sales department. I was ecstatic. Whether I could do the job properly or not was beside the point; I got the job. Later on, I found out that the personnel officer used to be in the army and he was in Japan and had worked with Japanese employees. He knew that Japanese people were hardworking and very, very honest so he gave me a chance. How lucky I was. That was my very lucky day!

I worked there for only a short time, actually, until I got an offer from the Japanese Consulate and I changed jobs. The Japanese Consulate was newly established in Sydney and I started to go to work at their office at Bellevue Hill.

I have been very happy in Australia because this country gave me freedom and my husband gave me freedom to do what I wanted — go to work and also study. I was not oppressed. I could speak up and say what I wanted to say. I did not have to look at my husband's expression of 'You must stop talking or keep your mouth shut.' And he was never the speaker on behalf of me.

I did meet a few Japanese people. One particular young Japanese couple, I will never forget. The husband was the representative of a big Japanese shipping company and his wife was a very charming lady. They came to visit us at home one day. The husband did not give any chance for his wife to open her mouth. He did all the talking. I wanted to talk to his wife but it seemed that she would not be allowed to open her mouth at all. I thought to myself, Poor her. What was her husband worried about? Maybe he did not want his wife to get a bad influence from me.

I was born in Japan and I was brought up in Japan. I had a Japanese education. But I'm a naturalised Australian now. After living in Australia for so many years, in lots of ways I think like Australians. When people get married and adopt a new family name, it does not mean that they just forget the family that brought them up. And your sisters are still your sisters. My relations in Japan are still my relations. So, I should call myself Japanese–Australian.

I love Australia very much and I'm lucky to be here. When I arrived I was told about Australians hating the Japanese and all that, but one to one they never attacked me. I never experienced racism. There has only ever been one incident and that was very recently. Only last year an older lady abused me in a shopping centre car park. She thought I was going to steal the parking spot that she had an eye on. She got out of the car and told me to go home, go back to China. What's the use of arguing with someone like that? That was the only time I was verbally abused in Australia and it was after Pauline Hanson formed the One Nation party.

Only last year an older lady abused me in a shopping centre car park. She got out of the car and told me to go home, go back to China.

The Education of a Communist

The tale of Chris Gatz

In 1941, after the Greek Communist Party formed the National Liberation Front (EAM) and its military arm, the National Popular Liberation Army (ELAS), other, smaller Greek resistance groups started up. Most notable was the National Republican Greek League (EDES) which was supported by the British.

Working together, EAM/ELAS and EDES were responsible for many daring acts of resistance. But, as World War II drew to an end, things changed. There was no longer a common enemy. EAM/ELAS and EDES started to fight each other for postwar power. During the winter of 1943–44, civil war broke out and soon Greece was at war again; but this time the enemy was within.

A twelve-year-old shepherd boy, Chris Gatzastras, was one of the many victims of this tumultuous time in modern Greek history.

* * *

I was born in a small village called Vissani-Pogoniou, which is in the north-western part of Greece, about thirty kilometres from the Albanian border. This is a real typical Greek village where most of the people survived by toiling the land and having sheep and goats. My family is large: six boys and three girls. We come from a *Vlach* family — shepherds, in other words. We speak an ancient Latin language called *Vlachika* as well as Greek. At home we spoke strictly *Vlach* and outside we spoke Greek.

I was born on 20 February 1937 and some events that happened when I was about three or four years old have stuck with me ever since. I remember one early morning in 1940 when we heard this thundering noise, like lightning. All the people in the village were looking out of their houses and panicking. No one knew what was happening. The village was so remote that we didn't have any telephones or radios or anything like that.

The next day, we saw in the village these strange-looking

people, dressed in different clothing and speaking a different language. They set up camp right across from the village and they started lighting fires and cooking their meals. They took quite a few chickens and sheep from the villagers. But they were not aggressive. They were young people and they were singing and dancing, as if nothing happened. This was the Italian invasion of Greece on 28 October 1940.

These people camped there for a few days, then they started heading for the provincial capital, Ioannina. They didn't get more than ten or fifteen kilometres before they came to the Greek defence line of Kalbaki. There was a very big battle and the Greek Army put the Italians on the run. A lot of young Italian soldiers died in our village. While they were withdrawing, they left a lot of guns and grenades and army equipment lying around.

When I was about eight years old I was playing with my two younger brothers, Sotiris and Niko, when I found one of the leftover hand grenades. I thought it was a toy or something. I remember that there was some red colour on it and I wanted to remove the red, so I took a rock and started hitting the grenade. It exploded. The legacy of that was that I nearly lost my life. I lost a few fingers and I had many injuries on my face and chest, but the worst thing was that I lost my eyesight completely, because a lot of shrapnel went into my eyes. It took a long time before I got some of my sight back. This incident happened in late 1945, after the war.

A few months after the Italian invasion, again we saw some strange people talking a strange language and dressed in a strange way come into the village. But this time these people were more abrupt, more arrogant, and they surrounded the village. They gathered all the villagers into the centre of the town and sorted out the young men from the old people and the children, then they took all the young men away. I remember that one man tried to escape and he was quickly shot. This was the first time that we actually saw someone from our village get killed.

The next time the Germans returned, they burnt about twelve of the best houses in the village. This was 1942–43 and there was already a Greek Resistance army fighting the Germans.

A village next to ours, called Medzidie (Kefalorriso), where my mother came from, was occupied by Vlach shepherds who were taking part in the resistance. The Germans went there, took thirty-two able men, put them together in a house and burnt them alive.

This sort of thing went on for years. You must understand that, in those years, we were all very, very poor — destitute. There weren't any food supplies coming from anywhere, so every villager tried to survive any way they could. In the big cities like Athens a lot of people died from hunger. We were lucky because we had sheep, goats and some little plots in the mountains, where we could plant some wheat. Our daily food was porridge: flour mixed with boiled water, or with milk if we were lucky.

At the end of about 1944, when the Germans were kicked out of Greece, everybody seemed to be very, very happy. I remember that day because the church bells rang all day and everybody was so happy. So we thought, That's it. Good days will come from here on. But unfortunately that wasn't to be. Worse days were to come. Much worse.

We didn't know anything about communism, we didn't know anything about democracy. Almost everyone in the village was illiterate. There was one elderly person in the village who would read the news to the rest of the neighbourhood.

I remember that the real problems started in the early months of 1945, when the Greek Government in exile was supposed to have elections. Instead of this being worked out in a peaceful and friendly manner; the real witch-hunts started. This time the enemy wasn't wearing strange clothes or speaking a strange language or looking different. This time it was Greeks against Greeks — the worst possible situation.

Elements of the extreme right, including German collaborators and fanatical monarchists, formed a paramilitary group called the 'X' hites. Out of fear that the communists might take over the country, they started prosecuting those who were communists in the Greek Liberation Army (ELAS) and those who were fighting, those who were hiding arms. They went from house to house, picking up young men who served in the Resistance.

I vividly remember Easter of that year. On one nice day the whole village had a picnic near the village monastery. The entire town was celebrating and drinking. They were having real, real fun and it was the first and the last time in my life that I ever saw my father so happy.

Months later, in March 1946, the literate man was reading the news to the villagers, including my grandmother, who was the one holding our household together. He was telling them that in a Macedonian village called Litohoro there was a new communist fighting movement called the *Andartes* — which, in Greek, means guerrillas. This group was retaliating against the 'X' hites, going to villages, pillaging and burning houses. They were going after anyone they thought to be right wing. They had killed a priest and they were committing a lot of atrocities and the regular army was fighting them.

The guerrillas were spreading fear right through the countryside of Northern Greece by answering terror with harsher terror. The fear started in our village because these guerrillas were getting closer to where we lived. We didn't know what to do. A lot of people in the village who felt they might be prosecuted by the communists packed up and moved south to the army-protected areas.

My father didn't want to move. As he put it, 'Look, we went through the Italians, we went through the Germans and now why should I leave the village because of my own people? Where would I go? I've got a big family. I can't go. I'll just stay here and take whatever comes.'

But my Uncle Kosta, my mother's brother, kept saying to him, 'Pano' (Panoajoti was my father's name). 'Take your family, move south, because things are very bad. These people are coming and they probably want to forcibly conscript your older son, Michio.'

My father used to say to him, 'My son is only sixteen years old, for God's sake. Surely they're not going to take him.'

One day the communists came to our village and forcibly conscripted two older shepherds, but my father still didn't believe that they would take my older brother until they returned. They surrounded the village and, with a list of names in their hands, they went from house to house, forcibly conscripting boys and girls from the age of fifteen. Most of these never returned home. They were killed in the battles of Gramos and Vitsi at the closing conflict of the Greek Civil war in autumn 1949.

They took my brother. They gave him a bit of training.

They took my brother. They gave him a bit of training. In a battle he was caught by the paramilitaries and they killed him. They didn't just kill him; they mutilated him and left him to die.

In a battle he was caught by the paramilitaries and they killed him. They didn't just kill him; they mutilated him and left him to die. This happened very early in 1947 and for a long time after, we were asking the other guerrilla parties that used to come to the village, 'Have you seen Michio?' And they would say, 'Yes, yes. He's there, he's doing this, he's fighting . . .' All the while they knew he was dead and they were lying to us. That was another reason why my family never moved south: we were always hopeful that Michio would one day return.

Our village was in the middle of an area that, on one side of the river, was controlled by the army and on the other side was controlled by the guerrillas. The period between 1945 and 1948 was a very interesting time because even close relatives — and I mean close relatives, like my father's own first cousins, whose houses we used to go over to on a daily basis — all of a sudden found themselves alienated from my father, all because of politics. My father never joined, or got involved in, any political party or resistance. He was busy with his large family — all under the age of sixteen, with Michio the eldest.

Where before you had a loving village, where people used to have their own sheep and goats and their little plots next to one another and they used to help each other and sing and laugh together, now, all of a sudden, they couldn't even speak to each other. They didn't trust each other. It was friend against friend, brother against brother. It became a very, very strange place.

I remember, in the summer of 1948, there was a big army push from the south and I was with the shepherds and my older brother Nashio. In summer the shepherds usually sleep during the day and look after the sheep at night. That particular day was very hot and very beautiful and we started hearing a lot of thundering noise, artillery fire and gunfire, and then nothing. Suddenly the gunfire started again and then, a few minutes later, we saw a guerrilla coming. He was wounded. He was carrying an overcoat and he had a machine gun. He ordered my father to take the overcoat and follow him.

I was only eleven at the time, but already I knew that, if they take somebody away, they conscript him and you never see him again. As this guerrilla was taking my father and they were about fifty or a hundred metres away, something came into my mind very quickly. I ran after them, tapped my father on the back, grabbed the coat and whispered to him, 'Turn back.'

I followed the guerrilla up into a valley that went into an open field. When we reached the open field, the army from the other side of the valley noticed two people. They started shooting at us with machine guns. The bullets were going '*ppsht ppsht ppsht*' just on top of us and the leaves were falling from the trees. So the guerrilla turned back and said to me, 'Sit down, get down!' And when he turned around he saw that it was me instead of my father and he said, 'Where's your father?'

I said to him, 'He's back there.'

Obviously he didn't have much time to discuss things because the bullets were coming down and he said to me, 'Just follow me.'

At a church outside the village he met a group of guerrillas and as they started talking amongst themselves, I ran back, without any shoes. When I finally got back to where I had left my father, everyone, including all the sheep and goats, had already left, so I got really frightened. At the time we were grazing in another village called Stavroskiades, about six kilometres from the Albanian border. I was screaming and yelling and crying, because I thought they had gone there and abandoned me.

This went on for a few minutes and then I heard my father say, 'Christo, I'm here.' And when my father saw me he started crying from happiness. He took me and then we ended up in a village called Drimades, close to the Albanian border. There we met my grandmother and my father left me with her. The rest of our family was left behind in our village: my mother and six children, the youngest being a month old.

We slept one night at a camp near the Albanian border. In the morning we realised that there were more than two thousand villagers there. It was the headquarters of the guerrillas and they had an open field hospital there. Early in the morning a reconnaissance plane flew over. It wasn't a communist plane because the communists didn't have any planes. It did two circles and left. They didn't shoot at us or anything. But a couple of hours later we started hearing artillery fire on top of us and people started running, trying to hide here and there. Some people were killed. We got scared and we rushed in through the Albanian border, thinking that the next day we could come back again.

I vividly remember this old lady — this very old, very poor, destitute lady on the other side of the border. She had no shoes on and she was sitting on the rooftop of a low barn. And as I was going past, with my grandmother holding me by the hand, this old lady said to my grandmother in Greek, 'You poor souls, where do you think you are going?'

In Albania there was already the communist system and they lived not in poverty, but below poverty. Below, below poverty. They had less than nothing. This place was mostly settled by Greeks and belonged to Albania. We called it Northern Epiros; and the region I come from, Epiros. We thought we were still in Greece.

We were taken to a small town called Argyrocastro and placed in a mosque. In the hall of the mosque there was

When it got dark, this man came and put three light bulbs in and turned them on. When we wanted to go to sleep the old ladies stood in front of the bulbs and tried to blow them out. One of them was blowing and blowing, with the other saying, 'Blow a bit harder, harder!'

nothing; it was just stone. We stayed down there for two months and that was the only thing Albania could offer us. I'm not ungrateful, because they were very, very poor.

I remember that we were so naïve that, on the first night, when it got dark, this man came and put three light bulbs in and turned them on. When we wanted to go to sleep the old ladies stood in front of the bulbs and tried to blow them out. One of them was just blowing and blowing, with the other saying, 'Blow a bit harder, harder!'

And she was saying, 'I am blowing hard but it just won't go out.'

The man who had put up the lights was watching this from the far corner of the hall and called out, 'Look, I'm going to blow it out for you.' And he switched off the lights.

The two old ladies said, 'How did you blow it out from all the way over there, when we couldn't from here?'

All these villagers, all these poor people, had never seen a light bulb before. They had never seen a telephone, they had never seen anything, in those days. We were all from very remote parts of Greece. What did we know? Now, they have everything, but then it was a different story.

In 1949 the Greek communists formed a committee and they decided to send thousands of young Greek children in Albania to other communist countries. We were seen as young political refugees and they were going to send us where we could get schooling and everything that we needed — everything that Albania could not provide for us. The Greek Communist Party had plans for us: we were supposed to take control of the future People's Republic of Greece that never eventuated.

My father didn't want to let me go, but I wanted to go because, when we first landed in Albania, we went to a hospital and a doctor examined me and he said to my grandmother, 'If you take this kid to a hospital he probably will get back more of his sight.' And because I overheard that, I thought I'd better go because these people would do that for me.

I begged my grandmother to let me go. I can still remember vividly when the committee came and put us on the back of horses to take us away. My grandmother was crying her eyes out and she said, 'I'll never see you again.' But I promised her that I would see her again because I was young and I never thought that this would be the last time. I remember how she let me go, how she kissed me goodbye. She was right: that was the last time I ever saw my grandmother. I never forgave myself for not keeping my promise to her. Of all the children, I was the closest to her.

I finally ended up in Budapest, Hungary. And there it was like going from hell to paradise. We were only young kids and virtually as soon as we arrived in Hungary we were given brand-new, beautiful clothes, which we had never seen in our lives before. You know what it means to have a nice clean shirt, trousers and shoes! We didn't know what shoes were.

The Hungarians let us stay in a beautiful building that the communists took from the rich people and nationalised when they came into power. These buildings were turned

We were so naïve, we didn't know where to sleep. We didn't know whether we had to sleep under the mattress, under the sheets or under the blanket. Some of the boys went under the bed!

into children's homes and suchlike. They put us in dormitories and each one of us had his own bed, with nice sheets, a blanket and a mattress. We were so naïve, we didn't know where to sleep. We didn't know whether we had to sleep under the mattress, under the sheets or under the blanket. I remember some of the boys went under the bed! And then we had five meals a day. In the morning: milk, bread and marmalade. At 10 o'clock we had toast with marmalade. And then we had three proper meals. We thought this was paradise. We thought, This is it. Whatever you want to call it, so be it. If this is communism, it can't be bad. It has to be good, very good.

Soon after we arrived they put us in school. All I had in Greece was about two years of primary school — nothing else — and I was now nearly twelve years old. That's where, you could say, a slow, gradual and very, very successful indoctrination into the communist ideology started. They didn't have to tell us very much. They didn't have to tell us 'You must believe this'; we accepted it, even if the utopian concept of communism was more or less wishful thinking. We believed in a world where everybody would be happy and everybody would have plenty and everybody would be treated the same, regardless of race or nationality. Plus we didn't have any contact with the world outside the school grounds, so we didn't know exactly how the Hungarians lived. We assumed the Hungarians under the communist system lived better than us. So we didn't have any comparison, except for what we remembered from Greece and that was pure hell.

I vividly remember one particular day when I was in high school. Our school principal called me into his office and when I got there he started questioning me about some very strange things. He asked me over and over, 'Do you have relatives in the West?'

And I said to him, 'Comrade,' — because there you call everyone 'Comrade', no matter how old or how young the person was — 'why are you asking me this?'

He said, 'Do you have somebody in Australia?'

I said, 'Australia? All I know about Australia is what I learnt in Geography. Who do I have in Australia . . . ?' And he was more or less insisting, and I was protesting that I didn't, until finally he gave me a letter addressed to me from Australia.

I opened the letter and inside were a couple of photos and a letter written in Greek. The letter was from an uncle. He was telling me 'I'm your Uncle George, I'm your father's brother and I left Greece in 1927, I migrated to Romania and from Romania I came to Greece, but when I came to Greece, Greece was war torn so I decided to migrate to Australia in 1950.' From that moment on I kept contact with my uncle and he was writing to me about Australia and how good it was and how prosperous.

My Uncle George lived under the Romanian communist regime for just on three years. He had his own restaurant which was taken over by the new communist government, so, together with his Hungarian wife and daughter, he managed to get repatriated to war-torn Greece in 1947. He couldn't get in contact with us at the time because we were under guerrilla control.

It was a strange time because, all of a sudden, I discovered that I had an uncle whom I didn't know existed, let alone one living in another country, which happened to be a capitalist country. That, of course, didn't look very good — either in my eyes or in the communists' eyes.

In 1953 my family in Greece was not doing too well. My older brother was in Albania with all the sheep and goats. My father was in exile in southern Greece after escaping from Albania. My mother had six children and no source of income because the sheep and goats were with my brother, so she was working with my fifteen-year-old sister in the fields. I wanted to do something to help them, but from communist Hungary that was impossible, so Uncle George in Australia suggested that I come to Australia. He was insisting that if I came here I would really be able to help my family.

At that time I was very strongly indoctrinated in the communist ideology. I really believed in it, with all my innocence, so I was in a real personal dilemma: I had to help, but if I left Hungary I was betraying my beliefs, betraying the system, betraying everything. Then again, I thought, What the heck, the communists aren't only here, they're supposed to be all around the world. What's the difference if I am here or I'm there? I'm a communist and I'm not going to change.

So finally I decided, in the winter of 1955, to take my uncle's offer and migrate to Australia. But the problem was: how do I get a passport? I managed through some friends secretly to approach a French Legation in Budapest that represented the Greek Consulate in Paris and to apply for a passport. And then I waited. I waited a few months and nothing happened, so I thought, Forget it, it's impossible.

In high school we had a system whereby the more politically orientated students took it in turns to read all the daily news and talk about it with the other students after dinner, like a group discussion of world events. One evening it was my turn to do that and the principal was there. After I had led the discussion the principal said to me, 'Comrade, have you completed what you have to say?'

I said 'Yes.'

And he said, 'Are you sure you covered everything?'

Again I said 'Yes' and he said, 'Well, I don't think you covered everything, but anyway I want you to come and see me in my office.'

I thought nothing of it but on my way to the office one of my fellow students, a Greek, said to me, 'Christo I didn't have a chance to tell you, but earlier today the principal asked me to come to his office and he gave me a letter to read and it is a letter from the Greek Foreign Ministry directed to you, through the French Legation.'

Nobody was supposed to know — it was my secret. When he mentioned that, I really got scared. I went to the principal's office. He sat me down and gave me a serious dressing down. It was like, 'Why do you want to leave? We are providing you with everything.' And why this and why that.

After about twenty minutes I said to him — and I really believed this, 'Comrade I'm leaving the country not because I don't like the system or because I am anti-communist. In fact, I am very, very proud to be one. Besides, the communists are not only needed here, the communists will be needed more down there where the capitalists are, to make them understand! So I don't see anything wrong in wanting to leave.'

Apparently the letter had arrived about a week earlier. The principal had got instructions from the high authorities to dismiss me from the college because of what I had done and put me in isolation. Isolation meant that I was not to be in contact with the rest of the students. But still I did not waver from my own ideology. Even when I was put in isolation, I accepted it, because privately I thought, Yes, I am doing something wrong by leaving the communists and going to the capitalist world.

Eventually I got all my papers in order and I left Hungary by train, heading for Trieste. On 29 June 1956, I boarded the Italian ship *Toscana* for Australia. The ship was full of Italians, but I didn't know at the time that they were people migrating to Australia. I also didn't know that there were thousands of Greek people living in Sydney. I thought I was coming to a country with just my uncle and a lot of other foreign people here and I would have to start again — new language, new everything.

The first stop of the ship was in Brindisi, another Italian port, and from there we sailed through the Adriatic Sea, near the Greek Islands, which was one of the most emotional moments of my life. I could see the people saying, 'Grecia! Grecia!'

I knew then that they were saying, 'There is Greece! Look at Greece!' and I thought, Look, this is as close as I can get to my own country. God knows when I'll be able to come again.

On 13 August 1956, the ship approached Sydney Harbour.

When I arrived here my uncle and aunt were working and I stayed at home on my own for the first few weeks. Uncle George kept saying to me, 'Look son, the very, very first thing you have to do is learn the language. Without the language you can't move anywhere.'

So the first day that I was home by myself I turned on the radio and I heard this man talking in English. He was talking at one hundred miles an hour and I thought to myself, God, how am I ever going to learn this language?

This guy doesn't have an end or a stop on the words. I don't think I will be able to learn this language ever. I couldn't distinguish anything.

When my uncle came at night I said, 'Look, Uncle, I don't think I will ever learn this language, it's just too hard. I was listening to the radio and I couldn't understand anything.' My uncle switched on the radio and discovered that I had been listening to the horse races!

A few days after I arrived, my uncle took me to David Jones, because I really didn't have any clothes and he had said to me, 'Son, you better buy a double-breasted suit because you are only nineteen and here, unless you are over twenty-one, you don't get full pay. With a double-breasted suit you will look older.'

Then he wrote on a piece of paper, 'Have you got a job for me, please?' and said, 'You walk down Botany Road,' which was where a lot of Sydney's factories were, 'and wherever you see a factory or a place that looks like a factory you go there, knock on the door and just read them what is on this paper. If they have a job they will smile at you and will ask you to go in. But if they say sorry or something like that and they don't smile at you, you go and knock on the next door.'

I did that and eventually I got a job.

I had been in Australia only about a month when my Uncle George took me for a walk one weekend down to the Sydney Domain and there I saw people gathering, speaking freely on whatever subject they wanted to. I actually saw the Australian Communist Party's newspaper, *Tribune*, displayed openly and I didn't notice any harassment or any policemen hindering or stopping you from saying or doing whatever you wanted. I was surprised. How can this happen in a capitalist country? And that was really the beginning of my slow and gradual rethinking of the whole communist ideology. It wasn't easy because subconsciously I felt like I was questioning my own beliefs. It was like a self-betrayal. You could say it was the gradual debriefing of one's belief.

Later on, I myself had to think as a capitalist and act as a capitalist when I became self-employed and then an employer. And it was then that I started to ask, Where is a person more free? Is it really under the communist ideology or is it here? Because here I've had every opportunity to do whatever I wanted. There was no law to stop me getting involved with any kind of business. It was up to me.

So for me that thing of capitalism which, in the beginning, I hated as being the evil of mankind, turned the other way around completely. I began to see that, if a person is willing to work and work hard, he gets rewarded regardless of what sort of work he does, whether he is in a small or big business. If you work honestly and do the right thing you will make it in this life.

This coming August I'll be forty-five years in this country. I have not collected one day's unemployment benefit yet and it's very unlikely that I will get it now, because I am a self-funded retiree. I contributed to this country in my own way, with my own taxes and with the people I employed in my business, through all these years. Australia has never had to pay one single dollar for my upkeep. I still pay taxes and I will still be paying taxes till the day they bury me, thank you very much. And I'll pay gladly, because you have no idea how nice it is not to have the thunder of cannons, the bombardments and the fear of war around you all the time. As soon as I landed in this country everything seemed so beautiful. The only time I hear explosions in this country is New Year's Eve — and then it's the sound of peace, not war.

I hope that my children, Christina and Angelo, and my grandchildren, Stephanie and Anna, will live on and enjoy the foundations that my wife Georgia and I have worked to set up. They are the lucky generation — to live in a time and a place of love and peace, which I hope will always be that way.

The only time I hear explosions in this country is New Year's Eve – and then it's the sound of peace, not war.

'If you don't tease the tiger, the tiger won't bite you'

The tale of Henry Sue

Left to right; mother, Ben(baby), Nancy, Henry, Susan (brother Malcolm not present).

In 1934, an army of 100,000 communists believed in Mao Tse-tung to the point of marching out of South China and marching 9700 kilometres to north-western China on a gruelling journey that was to last over a year. At the end, only a few thousand men were still alive and China was still a republic.

With the advent of World War II the Japanese, not the communists, became the real concern. Very early in the war, the Japanese seized the richest parts of China.

By the end of the war, in 1945, the communists had tightened their grip over China. After a bloody civil war, the new Chinese communist dictatorship was announced in September 1949. The government had a new chairman, Mao Tse-tung, and it became quite clear to Henry Sue's father that it was time for him and his family to leave.

* * *

I was born in China — Canton, China. I was about four years old when my family got out of China, through Macau to Hong Kong, because of communism. My father was a high commander in the Chinese Army, so when the communists took over we had no choice but to shift; otherwise my father would get into a lot of strife. It was a little bit like the *Sound of Music* situation, but not as glorified. In our case there was no car — we were on foot and tricycle. We had about fourteen pieces of luggage, large and small, and we escaped in the middle of the night through Macau.

I remember it was raining. We got a few tricycles in Macau. All the family and the luggage were loaded onto the tricycles and there was very little room to sit. In all of the confusion I was left behind. I thought, at that young age, Well, they probably haven't room for me. I guess I'll have to run at the back of the tricycle. But with my little legs it didn't take long for the tricycle to get away from me. I was crying and frightened.

People were running everywhere — people running scared in the dark and the rain — everybody shouting at everybody: 'Come on, come on, hurry up, get on the tricycle!'

We had to meet the boat, the ferry from Macau to Hong Kong. I didn't know what was happening. There was a lot of unrest in Macau at the time and a lot of people tried to kidnap young children and sell them, so being left alone was a horrible feeling for a young four-year-old boy. Luckily, my sister saw me running behind crying and called out, 'Oh, we left Henry behind!'

I had nightmares about that particular instance for at least ten years. I was always waking up in a sweat, dreaming that I was separated from my family. It was a horrific sort of feeling that remained with me.

When we got to Hong Kong there was hardship straight away because my father couldn't get a job. And we moved into the most dilapidated house with only one little room. At that time there were four of us kids and a husband and wife in two bunk beds.

Because of the desperation, my father soon became ill. In Hong Kong, when you get ill, the hospital costs a lot of money and in those days money was one thing we didn't have. To take things from bad to worse, we lived in a poor village in Hong Kong where all the houses were made of wood, but they weren't like wooden houses in Australia. The wooden houses over there are one next to another, like pigeonholes. So when one house gets on fire, it burns the whole suburb. I remember we were getting something at the bottom of the hill where we lived and we started to see this massive fire — fifty or sixty houses all burning at the same time. One of them was our house. Of our fourteen bags of luggage we recovered two bags.

It was a desperate time for my father and the family. Due to my father's army rank we had lived in a luxurious home in China. Then, when the army dissolved and through running away from communism to Hong Kong, we suddenly became exposed to poverty. Life became so hard and, with so many children in the family, my parents started wondering what they could do. My father decided the best choice was to sell a child — and I was the one.

My mother said, 'No, selling is not a good thing — what about just giving him to someone else so he doesn't starve to death?' It was my great-aunt who told me many years later that my mother refused to sell any of us. She'd rather we all die together than separate the family like that. It was in this moment of desperation that a letter arrived from one of my father's uncles in Australia. He had just opened a restaurant and wanted a hand, so he asked my father to come to Australia.

In those days, leaving your family behind was not a good thing. You didn't know where you were going and when you would ever meet again. But at the time my father had no choice: if he didn't go to Australia to try and find some way out, we would have all died.

When I was very young, I always wanted to study and was intrigued by people going to school. I was always watching young kids going to school and I asked Mum if I could go to school. But the money my father was sending from Australia wasn't much at all. It was barely enough for us to live on, definitely not enough for school fees. So Mum said, 'I can't afford to send you to school, son, but if you really want to go to school, what about I try to save enough money for you to go for one term. If you're really good at it, then perhaps you may be able to get some scholarship and study further. But as it is now, I cannot promise anything, Henry.'

After twelve months of struggling, Mum saved enough money and sent me for one term to the school. Then I got a scholarship and I only had to pay half the school fees and I

Mum kept saying, 'You have to go, son. Otherwise we are all going to end up in a pretty bad way. By going, you will give us hope later on. You have to be strong. You have to leave us.'

liked it. I was top of the class at school because, being from a poor family, people don't have to encourage you to study; you know how important it is that you get somewhere in education and find a better job to support your family.

Life in Hong Kong got harder and the money sent by my father from Australia wasn't enough, so we had to move back to Macau. We spent another four years in Macau, where I attended Shun Shiel school, run by the Presbyterian Church, again on a scholarship. By the time I was ten, things were again very desperate and my father asked my brother and me to go to Australia to assist in his new business. I didn't want to leave my family, especially my mother, as she had been very ill. I used to help her all the time, shopping and cooking for the family. I was very worried that she would not be able to look after herself and the rest of the family.

But Mum kept saying, 'You have to go, son. Otherwise we are all going to end up in a pretty bad way. By going, you will give us hope later on. You have to be strong. You have to leave us.'

We were torn between staying and going, but of course there was really no choice at the time. I would have preferred to stay and die with my family than leave them, but for the welfare of the family we had to leave.

My brother and I left for Australia from Hong Kong, on board the *Cheung Duck*, in January 1957. I was extremely upset at leaving my family and couldn't eat for some time. The next time I was to return to Hong Kong was in 1968, when I was twenty-one.

In those days, the airways were not that readily available for people without too much money so we came by boat. The boat took fourteen days. We were supposed to go to Brisbane, but we landed in Sydney because they didn't have a port in Brisbane to receive big ships. We stayed a day and then caught a train from Sydney to Brisbane. We didn't know what to expect from our father. The last time we'd seen him had been seven years before. We didn't know how he might have changed. We didn't know him.

When we arrived, my father was in Sydney to receive us. My expectation was that he'd say, 'Wow! Son, I missed you so much. I love you,' — those were the words I wanted to hear. But it was the contrary: he received us and patted each of us on the head and asked, 'How was the trip?' He then took us around the place and he said, 'This is Sydney, but that's not where we live — we live in Brisbane.' That was all the conversation.

My idea of Australia before I arrived was that I was going to go to school and I was going to help my dad a little bit. I thought that here I could get a little bucket and just dig up some gold and save enough money and send it back to my mum so she could come to Australia. I thought this was a rich country, because everybody back home always talked about it like that. I thought I would come to a place where there is milk and honey and gold — a very rich country, where you just reach out and you get yourself milk. It was just like heaven in my mind. That's my perception before I came to Australia and I did not know that I would have to work very, very hard.

When we arrived in Brisbane, my father said, 'Look, this is Australia and in Australia the culture is such that, when you are sixteen years old, you can leave home and be independent and look after yourself. Now you are ten years old, but you don't have that long to go — just another six years before you can be independent. I've been looking after the family for a long time now and I think it's time that you two buck yourself up and start working and sending money home.'

My brother looked at me and said, 'My God! What are we facing here?'

From that time forward, most of the money earned was sent to my mother in Macau. It was twelve years before the others were able to come to Australia. At times I'd live on bread and water, just to be able to send money over to them for birthdays and Christmas.

By the second week in Australia, I was already working in a restaurant. I was only ten years old.

Brisbane to me looked like an underdeveloped place, like a country town. The place where we came from in Hong Kong (and even in Macau) had high-rise buildings, traffic and lots of people. But here, you could walk throughout the whole city without meeting another Chinese person. Now they call Fortitude Valley 'China Town'. But in 1957/58 when you went to the valley, you didn't see any Chinese people and there were only about three restaurants. My uncle actually opened the first Chinese restaurant in Brisbane, called the Ti Tung Restaurant. I think it was the first Chinese restaurant in all of Queensland and that is where my father first worked in Australia.

My father and three partners then started another restaurant, Sea High, in Queen Street. At the time it was one of the biggest restaurants in the whole of Brisbane, maybe even Queensland. They employed eight kitchen staff, including five chefs and at least twenty waitresses. It was at the Sea High Restaurant that my brother and

I started to work when we arrived in Brisbane. Study was only a few hours a day; the rest was working and working.

In Brisbane we felt like we were deaf and dumb. What I mean is, people talk, but you don't understand, you don't know what they are talking about. You listen, but you don't hear anything and because you don't understand you live in fear all the time.

You're not only deaf, but you're also blind. Lettering on shops means nothing to you when you don't know a word of English. You don't know how to catch a bus or train. We actually walked from place to place. We were walking from where we were living in New Farm to the restaurant in Queen Street. It took us about half an hour. Later on we were taught how to catch a train, but we were still afraid that somebody might talk to us. When you go to the shop you don't know what to ask for, but if you're lucky, you see what you want and you point. So that was the situation — quite a frightening situation for a ten-year-old boy.

I remember one time my father asked me to go buy milk, eggs and butter. He said, 'Don't forget. "Milk, eggs and butter".' And he added, 'Don't worry, there is a corner store where there is a Chinese fellow called Peter Fong.' Mr Fong was married to an Australian lady, but he was mostly there in the shop and you could talk to him in Cantonese. My father said, 'If his wife is there you have to remember those words: "milk, eggs and butter".'

I said, 'Okay. Milk, eggs and butter.' And all the way to the shop it was 'Milk, eggs and butter. Milk, eggs and butter . . .' Well, with my luck, Mr Fong wasn't there. I walked into the shop and I saw the milk in the refrigerator and in the same compartment I saw the butter, but I didn't see any eggs. Suddenly I realised that I'd forgotten the word for eggs, so I went up to Mrs Fong and just went 'cluck cluck cluck', flapping my arms like wings, and I reached behind my bottom to show an egg being laid.

Mrs Fong was very clever and she said, 'Oh, eggs!' That was one of many times we got to use our sign language in those early days of life in Australia.

I realised very quickly that language is everything and I said to my brother, 'The first thing that we must learn is the language if we want to get anywhere around here.' So that's what we started to do — go to school and try to put our minds into learning English.

In those days, I would get up at six in the morning and catch two trains because my father managed to get us into a school that was a lot further than I expected from New Farm. It was in East Brisbane, at St Benedict's Convent, and it took two hours to get to school.

Already at primary school we found that a lot of kids, about a quarter to half of the class, were racially prejudiced. As soon as we started going, there were always loud chants of 'Ching Chong, Ching Chong Chinaman'.

When we finished our school day we had to catch two trains straight away, to get to Queen Street to work in the restaurant. By the time I got there, there would always be a mountain of dishes — pile upon pile on the floor, hundreds and hundreds of dishes. I was so small that they had to put a stool for me to stand on to wash those thousands of dishes. It was one of the busiest restaurants in the whole city. I remember how, when I hung the dishes on the dish rack, the water used to drip backwards. After the first half hour, all the water would be running down my arm, my body, my school pants, down to my shoes, and would fill my shoes with water. The water was very hot because of the greasy dishes and the detergent was very cheap, so every winter all my skin would crack and blood would come out. I would wash dishes every day non-stop for four or five hours until

We would get back from school and then work in Sue's Snack Bar from Monday to Thursday until midnight, then we would have to clean up. By the time we went to bed it was 1 or 2 o'clock in the morning.

about 10.30 or 11pm, then have some dinner and walk for half an hour to get home.

This went on for a few years until my father decided to buy a snack bar. So my brother and I started to work in the snack bar while my father continued in the Sea High restaurant.

He bought the snack bar not knowing that it was a hoodlum hangout, a bodgie hangout. In those days they called the rough, bad people 'bodgies'. This was the 1960s and the place was a bikie hangout. It had a juke box in the corner, banging out music all the time, and hoodlums coming in and making a lot of noise and spraying Coca-Cola everywhere. By the time we realised that we'd bought a bodgie joint, it was too late; nobody wanted to buy it back.

In the snack bar we were getting even more racial tension than in school! Every time we opened the door people would say, 'Get back to where you come from — we don't want you here. You're taking all our jobs, all our business.' You just ignore that and you go on, but it wasn't easy in those days. We would get back from school and then work in Sue's Snack Bar from Monday to Thursday until midnight, then we would have to clean up. By the time we went to bed it was 1 or 2 o'clock in the morning. On the Friday and Saturday we worked from midday till 2 o'clock in the morning, so by the time we got to bed it was 3 or 4 o'clock and Sunday we worked from midday to midnight. It was long hours — long hours to make just barely a living.

At that time, I hated Australia. I didn't think people were that friendly. I think that people made sure they reminded us that we were from Hong Kong — 'You're not one of us.' We found it very isolating in those days. I suppose missing my mother, sisters and brother in Hong Kong didn't help the way I felt about my life here.

The attitude among the hoodlums in those days was: If you want to eat and you haven't any money, you go to a Chinese restaurant. After they finished eating they'd just walk out and because the hoodlums were so big the Chinese restaurateur would be too frightened to ask for money. This was the common practice for uneducated Australians. I heard many stories of customers having a meal and walking out. The restaurateur would chase after them and say, 'Sorry sir, you've got to pay' and the customer would turn around and say, 'What! Don't bother me', and continue to walk away. The restaurateur would then say, 'Oh sorry sir, sorry sir', and that was it.

Right from the start, I said to my brother, 'We are not going to let that happen here — no way. We are not going to put up with that kind of rubbish, no matter how much abuse we get.' But there was nothing stopping a bikie or a truckie having a meal and then, when he was finished, saying, 'I didn't like that so I'm not paying', or 'That's not fillet steak — I'm not going to pay for that' and then walk out. Towards the end we got sick and tired of it, so (little as I was at sixteen) I said, 'We've got to start standing up for ourselves or we won't survive.'

We started to ring up the police and they would say, 'What's the matter — someone didn't pay? Well, it's not an important matter is it?'

Anyway, they'd take two or three hours to come and by

The Chinese have a philosophy. They say, 'If you don't tease the tiger, the tiger won't bite you.' But in Australia, even if you don't tease the tiger, the tiger still bites you. We found here that fighting was just another sport.

that time everybody would be gone. And when they did happen to arrive they'd say, 'Well, there is not much we can do for you, son. All you can do is give him your name and address and get his name and address, and you just sue one another.' And that was it! Well, running a small business, to sue one another you may as well forget it. Later on, we didn't even bother to call the police because we knew we were not going to get anywhere, so why waste time?

That's when we started fighting, fighting to survive. I was surprised that I started with Kung Fu because of my Christian family — my mother's mother, in particular, who is a real loyal Christian. We were brought up in a Christian family, in the Christian way of life. Fighting is seen as brutal and uncalled for. You don't fight. The Chinese have a philosophy. They say, 'If you don't tease the tiger, the tiger won't bite you.' But in Australia, even if you don't tease the tiger, the tiger still bites you. We found here that fighting was just another sport. So what? You just had a fight.

In those days, when you had a fight and the other person lost, they'd shake your hand and say, 'Good on ya, you're not doing too bad' or if you lost they'd say, 'Okay, try harder next time.' It was like a culture to them, but for us it was life and death. You don't fight unless you really have to — unless you have to protect yourself. So we found it was necessary to learn some kind of fighting to protect ourselves. The first necessity was to learn the language and the next necessity was to learn how to fight to protect our business, to protect our livelihood, so I guess that's how Kung Fu started. We had to learn how to fight quickly and in those days we got a lot of practice at Sue's Snack Bar.

Every window in the snack bar during our time there was broken three or four times. People would even throw dead cats through the door. No company wanted to insure the place. The bikies used to all park outside and they used to jump over the counter and fight on our side of the counter. It was just fighting all the time. People were even too afraid to walk past the shopfront.

I remember one fellow, he had a meal and finished the meal then said he was not satisfied with it. He had finished it except for one piece of noodle, one little piece of noodle inside the bowl. He said, 'Oh well, it's soggy. I'm not going to pay for this — it's soggy. I'm going.'

'No, you don't go,' I said. 'I'm going to call the police — if the police think that you don't have to pay for it — then you don't have to pay for it.'

He said, 'Are you going to stop me?'

I said, 'If you go like that I will be forced to stop you.'

So he said, 'You trying to be funny? Because I'm going to shove this whole plate down your throat.'

That's when I got a bit angry. I picked up his plate and smacked him right across the head with it, so he half fainted. I dragged him over to the counter here. He wanted to raise a punch, so I hit him and then chucked him on the counter. One of his mates tried to fight me from the back and I turned around and I smacked him. He crashed though the counter and started crying. His mate was a truckie, a very big guy, and I was very little (I mean I'm not big now, anyway).

There were about half a dozen of them in the restaurant and about another ten outside, waiting for action . . . and all against just the two of us boys.

The police came and they didn't understand who was fighting who. But the truckie was crying, so it was obvious he was the one who'd been fighting.

He said, 'I'm going to sue that guy. He's doing karate and he's doing jujitsu on me and judo.' But the word kung fu was not mentioned, so I said, 'No, I'm sorry, I'm not doing any of those sort of things.'

Even on my first day at high school I had a fight. I was so tired because I had been working at the shop, and on the first day someone pushed me and said, 'You've got to apologise — you just bumped me.'

And I thought, Come on, this is high school. I thought they would have more sense here. But this boy said to me, 'I'll give you two choices, Henry. Either you apologise or we fight on the oval at lunch.'

By this time, I was getting a lot of fighting practice at the snack bar and my fighting skills were already very good, so I actually blackened his two eyes. He could not come to school the next day and when he did come, he apologised to me.

He said, 'I told my father what I did and he said I deserved it. He said you don't pick on people like that.' This made me start to realise that maybe not everyone is bad, maybe we're just living in a very bad neighbourhood.

After a while, my brother and I had upset a lot of bikie gangs, so every time they lost a fight they would get another bikie gang and they would cause trouble. It accumulated until, one night, there were close to thirty bikies in the snack bar. That was the worst fight we ever had. They were meaning to tie us up, hang us up from the ceiling by our hands and then destroy everything in the kitchen. They tied ropes around the posts outside that held up the awning, then tied the ropes to the backs of their cars and tried to pull down the awning. That wasn't very successful, so next they all came in to start fighting. They wanted to humiliate us and thought that it would be very funny to bash us and hang us up. They were calling out, 'We're going to hang up you Chinamen' — and that included my father — 'from the ceiling.' I knew what was going to happen as my girlfriend at the time was the sister of one of the bikies and she had warned me.

So we just grabbed a bar, a stick — anything — as they started to come in. At first there were about half a dozen of them in the restaurant and about another ten outside, waiting for action . . . and all against just the two of us boys. One of them started by breaking a Coke bottle and then another, with a piece of four-by-two timber, started to smash everything. He was screaming, 'Get out of here, you bloody Ching Chong.'

Then the fight started. Armed with an iron bar each, we went haywire. We were whacking heads, legs, anything, and people start running everywhere. There was blood everywhere. For us that night was a life-and-death situation. To them it was just another game . . . until they saw we were just whacking them left, right and centre. There were broken heads and broken arms everywhere. The fight was eventually stopped when two police cars came.

We all went to the police station for questioning. The police wanted to know what happened, why were we always hurting people. Our explanation was, well we didn't ask for trouble, we don't go around looking for trouble. They came to us, they wanted to stop us from doing business. What were we supposed to do? All the police said was that if it didn't stop they are going to send us all back to Hong Kong.

When we eventually left the station at about 4 o'clock in the morning, waiting for us outside were ten of the bikies. They said, 'We'll get you one day', and they were swearing and carrying on. Well, we weren't afraid of them because we'd just had enough. We thought to ourselves, The worst they can do is kill us. We don't care if we get killed because it is no fun living anyway. It doesn't really matter.

When I was twenty-one years old I had my first holiday — a couple of weeks in Hong Kong. For the last eleven years I had had no days off. I worked seven days, seven nights, every week, every year. So eleven years on, I had saved enough money to go to Hong Kong to see my mother for the first time. When she asked me, 'How's your study?' I said, 'What study?' I was hugging my mother and crying. I said, 'What study? What future?' I just cried and cried. She asked, 'Do you like your life?'

I said, 'I hate my life. At one stage I was thinking about killing myself.'

So there was not much of a future because the fact was it was not much of a life. In Hong Kong and in Macau I used to be top of the class — I was always coming number one. That is why my mother was very disappointed that I wasn't given an opportunity to study in Australia.

I was so happy to see my mother again that I almost forgot how unhappy Australia had made me. I reassured her that I would do all I could to get the rest of the family to Australia. At that time it was very difficult for Chinese to immigrate here.

So I left my family again and returned to continue

working hard. All I could think of at the time was, When will all this trouble be over? How are we going to get out of this? I didn't have any real hope or goal at the time. I just wanted to get out of this mess and live like an ordinary person, to work hard and get somewhere in life. I didn't want any trouble. I needed to save enough money to get the rest of the family over.

For a long time there was no light at the end of the tunnel. Then my brother was getting married and that allowed us to bring the rest of the family to Australia. At last we would be together again. He then went about his own life and I was left with the business to run and the family to care for.

One day I decided that I was not going to persevere with the situation any longer and that I would change my life. The first thing I did was to get rid of the juke box. I then set about changing the snack bar into a restaurant. I repainted the whole shop, put carpet down, wallpapered the dining room and put in tables and chairs. The name was changed from Sue's Snack Bar to Sue's Café. I hoped that it would attract a different type of customer.

I started to have regular customers. The business got better and I realised that not all Australians were unkind and racist. Slowly, slowly, I started to see the light at the end of the tunnel. I started to see the possibility of making a place for ourselves in Australia after fifteen years of struggle, hardship and confusion.

When I changed our business, it changed our lives. We found that the business really took off. And it seems that one thing follows another. Because of the stability of the business, that encouraged me to seriously get into Kung Fu and start to teach it. And after fifteen years I started to have a day off — amazing! So on my day off I would to go to the Chinese Club in Brisbane and donate my time to teach Chinese children Kung Fu. This went on for a couple of years and the business grew and I got married and started to have kids.

The most important thing in my life at that time was still my mother and all my younger brothers and sisters, because by the early 1970s they were all here. My main objective was to help them finish their study. I wanted to give them the opportunity that wasn't given to me.

Happiness is not about seeking happiness for yourself. Happiness is helping others, especially the people you care about and love. Seeing them happy, seeing them fulfilled, you feel the inner satisfaction which no money can buy, so I set out to help all of them finish their schooling. My younger brother graduated as a civil engineer and my younger sister graduated as a nurse. My other sister graduated as a biologist.

There is a Chinese philosophy that says, 'You help yourself first and then you help your family and then you help your friend and then you help the world if you can.' In my case, I was yet to help myself.

For nearly twenty years, my life was on hold for the rest of my family. When they all had a career path to follow, I could set about my own plans. After setting up the restaurant and operating it for many years for the family, I finally bought it from my father so he could retire. Eventually I sold it and moved to the Sunshine Coast to open a large restaurant. All the way through, Kung Fu and restaurants were always managed hand in hand.

In 1988, after thirty-two years in the restaurant business, I retired from it and decided to put all my concentration into Kung Fu. I opened the Australian headquarters of the Chinese Kung Fu Academy on the Gold Coast. For the first few years it was very hard. I lost a lot of money and I asked myself, Why am I still sticking with it? The answer was simple: I love the art of Kung Fu and its philosophy.

Through teaching, people turn to you with their personal problems. By listening to them, I discovered that, be they Australian or Chinese, they have the same needs and suffer a similar sort of pain to what I'd been through. I realised that people are the same. People need people. People need to be cared for, need direction. I once needed help but nobody dared to help. Now, if there is somebody around that needs help, I will help him in any possible way.

During my first fifteen years here I was too involved with the hardship of survival. I was suffering. I never sat down to really count my blessings or see what was nice. I was indulging in my sad and sorry situation. I really didn't have time to look a bit further away from the environment I was in and see that there were a lot of nice people here who wanted to reach out and accept another culture. This is a very beautiful country to be in. We should all think of one thing: how to make Australia a better place for everyone living here.

I believe that Kung Fu not only teaches people to fight; it teaches people the correct way of living. It instils values, meaning and discipline. In martial arts, there are no racial differences because martial arts belong to the dedicated ones; they do not belong to a nation. They belong to the dedicated ones.

After my forty-three years of living, working and training in Australia and through teaching students of many cultures, I have learnt that people are basically nice. They all want to be accepted. If there is the slightest trace of racial discrimination, they are afraid of it. In order to minimise racial differences, one must try very hard to accept first and not wait to be accepted. Be open to others so that they will open themselves to you.

I am one who, at first, hated Australians. Now, I am proud to be an Australian. When one is not sure of who they are, there will always be reasons for not feeling accepted in a country. Racial tension will always occur to some extent. It is up to all of us to find a balance and help each other to do the same. I feel that, in Australia, everyone gets a fair go.

Through teaching, people turn to you with their personal problems. By listening to them, I discovered that, be they Australian or Chinese, they have the same needs and suffer a similar sort of pain to what I'd been through.

The Go-between

The Tale of Nicolas Habib

The ancient Egyptians had no caste system. Their society was divided into four social classes: royalty; artisans and merchants; workers; and slaves. A person from the poorest class could rise to the highest offices in the land without discrimination.

From the very beginning, the Egyptians were looking for the answers to the big questions. They were the forefathers of modern-day beliefs and ideals about humans, God and nature. What was critical in their culture was the relationship between people and society — concerns that formulated and directed the destiny of Nicolas Habib from the time of his birth in Alexandria, Egypt, in 1938 to the place he finally settled in: Melbourne, Australia.

* * *

In terms of nationality, I could consider myself a 'man without a country'. My father was Lebanese, my mother was of Greek Cypriot origin, I was born in Egypt and I went to a French school — so it is very hard to pinpoint my nationality. But I am proud of being of Lebanese and Greek origin and am amongst the original multicultural people. This has probably affected me, in that I don't see people in terms of their nationality, race or religion. And my French education always taught me to have wide horizons. When I meet a coloured person, I don't see black; I just see the individual. I might like him or I dislike him, but as far as colour is concerned, it doesn't mean a thing to me. That has been my upbringing, which of course formed my character and gave me a bit of idealism to strive for a better world.

At my school, St Marc College, I had alongside me people with Italian, Greek, Maltese, English, French parents — you name it, we had them. I had alongside me people of the Jewish faith, of the Moslem faith, Catholics, Orthodox, Protestants and we never differentiated one from another. We were just kids playing together.

My recollection of childhood is that it was a happy one.

Thanks to providence we were upper middle class, so our house was a whole building, shared with the business my father partly owned. My mother was quite a tough woman who came from a poor upbringing and always made us respect people, not because of their wealth but because they were human beings.

Well, Egyptian nationalism really started during the war. The English and the allied forces used us as pawns to stop the Germans and we thought that we would be rewarded with independence at the end of the war. We never were. The English persisted in occupying the country and it was only through blood and revolution that they left in 1947. But they maintained their presence in the Suez Canal.

After the war and the loss of Palestine in 1948, the pride of Egypt was hurt because Egypt was the biggest Arab country, having a population of about twenty million at the time. Therefore, as a child around 1948–49, I experienced two different levels of awakening. On one hand I remember seeing foreign nationals — Greeks, Maltese, Italians — leaving Egypt; and on the other hand, I witnessed refugees coming from Palestine into Egypt. That was the first time I became aware of the plight of refugees and it was maybe then, to some extent, that I was starting to form my political inclination — the love of the underdog, sympathy for the plight of people who didn't have the means to look after themselves and to defend themselves.

One day in 1949 about two or three thousand people demonstrated in front of our business where our house and showroom were. They were trying to destroy it, thinking it was a foreign business. Fortunately my father came down and talked directly to their leaders. They were extremely surprised that he spoke perfect Arabic and somehow, as soon as they found out that we were not a foreign company, they left us alone, but it was a very close shave.

In 1952 nine officers of the Egyptian Army decided to take over Egypt and on 23 July the Egyptian Revolution took place. We suddenly heard that martial law was declared and the King was on the way out. We didn't think that a group of officers would overthrow the King. That surprised us all and panicked us because a lot of people thought of the Egyptian Revolution as being a Marxist–Communist revolution. The foreign elements in the country felt that they would lose all their influence. So, from 1952 onwards, a period of great upheaval began. A lot of people panicked and left. Some of us in the foreign schools — like the French, English and Italian schools — started doubting our future. Where were we going to go?

A few months after Nasser took over, they started on an agrarian reform. And one of its biggest projects was the building of the Aswan Dam. Nasser immediately applied to get a loan from the World Bank, but the loan was refused, mainly on the grounds that Egypt was opening a relationship with Russia. So, in 1956, he nationalised the Suez Canal, as this represented $1 million profit per day. With the nationalisation of the Suez Canal and the subsequent attack by England and others, we were provided with a major dilemma. A key aspect was the limiting of our choice of jobs.

This was a crucial year for all foreign nationals living in Egypt. For me in particular it was even more serious. In 1952 my father had died so I gave up my university education and instead did a Diploma of Commerce. I started working in the family business after I graduated, in 1956, and then the government implemented some pretty harsh laws.

Opportunities to work for a reasonably high salary were very remote, so it was then that my decision to migrate started developing. My late mother left Egypt in 1956 because she already had a son in Australia. I was by myself. My first choice was to go to Lebanon, but Lebanon was in civil war. One of the places I would have liked to have gone was French Canada, because of my French education, but I had ties to Australia and Australia was really the country to go to.

Australia was advertised and promoted as a land of opportunity. My brother sent me the papers and, as he could offer accommodation, I started applying. But there were a couple of problems. First there was no Australian Embassy in Egypt because Menzies broke off diplomatic relations with Egypt at the time of the Suez Crisis. So I had to go to Greece to organise my paperwork. And there was a whole host of papers we had to get to come to Australia, like good contacts, good citizenship, no criminal record . . . But there were two particular documents that were required. One was proof of accommodation — you had to prove that someone would provide you with accommodation once you were in Australia. The other was proof that you were not a communist.

How can you prove you are *not* something? You can prove you *are* something . . . And no one would give me a paper saying that I was not a communist because, again, who cares if you are a communist or not? That delayed my departure to Greece by a couple of weeks and I was getting close to the day when I had to leave for Australia. Finally I decided to go to my school and say, 'For God's sake, give me a paper.' Being a Catholic school, they said that Nicolas was a good boy, he was not a communist, he was a practising Christian. And when I got to Athens that was good enough for the purpose.

In Athens we had to submit to all sorts of interviews to prove we were of good character. We were again asked the question 'Are you a communist?' To which I had to answer

I felt a bit left out because I wasn't qualified to be a non-skilled worker – I had never worked with my hands before – and there were no office jobs advertised.

'No.' It was quite funny because, when I came to Australia, I found that the communist party was a legal party. So that didn't make sense.

Finally I got the okay and, one morning in 1958, I got on the ship and headed towards Australia.

I knew Australia from books, from studying it, but mainly through the propaganda, the advertising and the leaflets. I thought of Australia as being a new country, still becoming established; attracting people to fill it up, as it was so big that it needed people; as a place with plenty of work and plenty of food of excellent quality. I think it attracted a lot of people like me with idealism, who believed we were going to a new country where we would find a job straight away. Also, our standard of living would be excellent, we would be eating meat every day and having that famous Australian butter that we used to pay dearly for in Egypt. I came in a British migrant ship and the perception was the same amongst the British migrants going to the land of the sun.

Well, when we arrived in Melbourne at Station Pier, the first impression was terrible. There was a shack as a milk bar and no facilities tourism-wise. There were big signs for non-skilled factory workers and machinists. I felt a bit left out because I wasn't qualified to be a non-skilled worker — I had never worked with my hands before — and there were no office jobs advertised, nothing clerical, which I found a bit strange. The other thing that shocked me was the standard of living, especially the tin roofs of the houses and those narrow streets of Collingwood — they really shook us.

With my Diploma of Commerce, I decided to look for office work, which of course was harder to get than non-skilled work. People didn't want office workers — they didn't expect migrants to apply for office jobs. They wanted us to be factory fodder — that's what they were after.

It took me two or three weeks to land a job. I had several interviews in hotels, in offices and I could see a bit of concern in their mind: How come you want office work? — a migrant, and a non-English migrant at that. I remember one particular personnel officer submitting me to a two-hour examination of maths and English, trying to convert pounds, shillings and pence into decimal currency without realising that, in Egypt, I knew about pounds, shillings and pence. After more than an hour of telling me I was very good, he said I needed to get local experience and then I could have a job. But how I was to get local experience was another story.

I remember, the first week I arrived here, that my brother decided to take me by train to the city to have a look at Myer's. Everyone went to Myer's the first day they arrived and I remember vividly now that I dressed in the morning in a very light grey suit and black and white shoes with a stiletto type of style. When I came out of the bedroom, my brother, who was five years older than me, looked and said, 'Are you coming to the city like that?'

I looked at myself and I said, 'Why, what's wrong?'

And being a practical joker he said, 'Oh well, fair enough.'

Anyhow, we went to the city by train. I landed in Flinders Street and the whole street was looking at me. It was very, very embarrassing. Then there were some unfamiliar words mentioned — the equivalent of 'gay' but a bit harsher at that time — and it was quite an experience. When we got back home, it was explained to me that people didn't dress modern. So that was a shock to the system also.

Another time, a good friend of mine who was working at the Taxation Department rang me and said, 'Nicolas, I've met a lovely girl here and we can go to the beach together and she will bring a girlfriend with her.'

So, fine. We spent the day with those two girls on a South Melbourne beach and it was lovely. Then one of them was kind enough to invite us to her house, which was the first time we had gone to any Australian girl's house. We were very proud of it. The parents were there, which we found a bit unusual. I mean, meeting the parents of a girl in our culture was at a very serious stage and this was only our first get-together.

They were very pleasant and we stayed for dinner and they had silverside. I remember the sliced silverside: you could see through it. The father was served first and he took one slice of silverside. With it he had beetroot and lettuce and carrot.

I thought to myself, Well, Nicolas, that's entrée — that's probably the first taste.

So I took exactly the same quantity as the father: one piece of silverside, one piece of lettuce, one beetroot and one carrot.

Then the mum came and said to the father, 'Would you like some more dear?' And the father looked and said, 'Oh no, no. I'm full.'

It was a time when we could eat a whole leg of lamb by ourselves, as far as our appetite was concerned. But I thought, I'd better be polite. Let's do like the Romans do. So

> Basically, the idea of assimilation for people coming from Egypt was very foreign. For myself, coming from mixed parents, I was always taught to be proud of my two thousand years of culture.

when I was asked did I want any more, I looked at the mother and said, 'Oh no, Mrs (whatever her name was), I've had enough. I'm full, too.'

And I was starving. We came to the end of the meal and the mother said, 'Alright boys. Nicolas, you wash the dishes. And Charles, you wipe.' Which again was a shock because we'd never washed plates in our lives, as men, and certainly not as guests. But we had to do it. Then we had to get out of the place very, very quickly to get to the milk bar for a couple of sandwiches!

That was our first introduction to an Anglo–Australian house. Of course, things have changed since.

At the time, Australia was quite a culture shock to us, especially coming from Egypt. There, all the various ethnic groups lived quite comfortably with each other: Greeks, Italians, Maltese, French . . . And coming here, we suddenly discovered that there was an assimilation policy. We were meant to become Anglo–Australian and we hadn't realised that when we arrived. I mean, personally, I was under the impression that I was coming to a new country, that was being built up. We were expected to forget about our language, our custom, our culture and become Anglos — and I think that hurt us a hell of a lot.

Basically, the idea of assimilation for people coming from

I remember visiting someone at Larundel Psychiatric Hospital and seeing an eight-year-old girl translating for the doctor the psychiatric problems that her mother had.

Egypt was very foreign. For myself, coming from mixed parents, I was always taught to be proud of my two thousand years of culture. Suddenly, coming here, we felt that a nation of one hundred and fifty years was telling us how to behave and not taking advantage of what we brought in. Whenever I mentioned that I spoke five languages, people said 'So what?' Well, I think that influenced my activities in later years in becoming an activist on multiculturalism.

So people formed EEAMA, an organisation which was basically a league of Greeks from Egypt and the Middle East whose main purpose was to provide a social umbrella and a place where our language could be spoken, our culture maintained and our food served, and where kids would meet so that children could intermarry and keep the culture alive. And of course it was assimilation that forced a lot of migrants to create organisations and pressure groups so as to survive in this atmosphere. Another example was the Australian Greek Welfare Society, whose purpose was to maintain the Greek identity. This led to a complete transformation from the days of the assimilation policy to what is now known as multiculturalism and into the transformation of this country, making it a beautiful and wonderful country actually.

Being multilingual was not recognised officially and to some extent you were taken advantage of as a worker. It was years later, mainly as a result of pressure from activists, that this was recognised as an extra skill. Even our public institutions, like hospitals, suffered. I vividly remember visiting someone at Larundel Psychiatric Hospital and seeing an eight-year-old girl translating for the doctor the psychiatric problems that her mother had. I mean, the possible consequences were beyond belief. I think that influenced me in some of my later work quite a bit.

The same with banks, the same with government departments, and so on. You brought someone — your kid or someone — to translate for you. I think it took years and years for the Government to recognise that that was not the ideal set-up.

The first time that I became aware of it from a commercial point of view was with the banks. The banks had a migrant advisory service where they would hire people with knowledge of languages and they would book them tickets on the migrant ships from Fremantle, which was the ships' first port of call in Australia. These people had the job of recruiting migrants into banking with the particular institution. So that was the beginning of the interpreter's service.

There was a question of qualifications. They told us nothing about non-recognition of qualifications or of past experience, and that's why a lot of us got a bit of a shock. I remember one of my supervisors, an early Hungarian refugee from Eastern Europe named Frank Kelemen. He had a PhD in Economics from the Sorbonne, but to Australians this was a completely unknown little university. (Of course, it happens to be one of the finest universities in the world.) His first job was to put charcoal onto railway wagons and I remember saying to him, 'Frank, weren't you hurt by doing that work?'

And he said, 'Well listen, young man. Australia didn't

A lot of non-Anglo migrants were being pushed to assimilate during that period. But the more they were pushed, the more the migrants were withdrawing into their own circles and failing to participate.

bring us here for our qualifications or our good looks. They brought us here because they wanted factory workers, factory fodder. So that's why we have to put up with it — we've got no choice.'

I think for the qualified, professional type it was pretty hard. But for the tradesman and people skilled with their hands, it was different.

English being the only widely used form of communication here certainly produced a lot of frustration in many migrants. That's why people gathered together with their compatriots, lived in suburbs where the others all lived. In the factories they assembled into nationality groupings and later on they elected union representatives for each national group.

Strong links were formed between the various migrant groups. Italians became very close to the Greeks, the Greeks to the Yugoslavs, and so on. Suddenly you felt more secure amongst other foreigners than you did amongst the locals and it became 'us and them'. You often heard amongst migrants the expression 'Oh, he's an Australian.' In other words, don't trust him; or, he doesn't understand you and vice versa. Although each migrant nationality was so different, Anglo-Australians always grouped us into one. To them, we were all migrants. Whether you were Greek, Italian,

Yugoslav, Arab or Turkish didn't matter — you were a foreigner, a migrant.

A lot of non-Anglo migrants were being pushed to assimilate during that period. But the more they were pushed, the more the migrants were withdrawing into their own circles and failing to participate. It was like Australia was insulting their culture, their identity. Well, I didn't take that stand; instead I kept on thinking that there must be a way of bridging the two: on the one hand, for migrants to accept that they were in a host nation that was providing work and food; and on the other hand, for the host society to accept that, when you invite people to come to your land, you have to help them to adjust to the new culture and to build a nation from that fusion. As a result, we started developing the idea of ethnic clubs, first to provide welfare to Australians of Greek origin, then to put pressure on the Government to allow more for migrant welfare, to organise interpreting services, to provide interpreters in hospitals and to explain government policy to migrants.

As a result, I started doing a lot of voluntary work, interpreting for people at the doctors or taking them to court and so on. A lot of solicitors who heard of my language skills used me to translate for their clients. I put my name up at the Richmond Police Station, saying that if someone was charged from the ethnic community, they could call me at any time and I'd interpret for them. And through that sort of network, I made wonderful friends. I joined the Good Neighbour Council, which in those days was a bit patronising and made up of Australian old ladies attending naturalisation ceremonies and serving cups of tea to the migrants.

At that time, I thought the biggest problem in Australian society was the lack of interpreting facilities. God knows how many wrong medical decisions were taken through

Extremism on one side
brings extremism on the other side.

wrong diagnosis or how many legal cases were lost because of a wrong brief. So I became vicious on that subject. I joined the Labor Party and started putting motions for interpreting facilities. I started asking why the English migrants who had just arrived in this country got the right to vote while the Greeks and Italians did not have the right to vote. After all, we were all foreigners and there was such a thing as Australian citizenship. It was these incidents that began firing my activism and my idealism.

Extremism on one side brings extremism on the other side. In 1969, when I was working at General Motors, we had a strike that lasted several weeks. Then there was the big struggle of 1973 at the Ford Motor Company. As eighty-nine per cent of the Ford workers were migrants, it affected migrants. Violence occurred, disagreements exploded into conflict. The unions did not understand migrant requirements because they lacked cultural awareness, just as the employer did, so there was a big division between the shop stewards, who represented the migrant workers, and the union officials.

The union and Ford would agree in an Anglo way amongst themselves, but when the union went back to the migrant workers, they would find that the ambitions and desires of those workers were not represented. In the end, the frustration became so great that it led to open violence. For example, migrants couldn't understand the idea of ambit claims. If the union asked for a $30 rise, the employer offered $6 and the final outcome was $10, the workers thought they were being exploited because they didn't get their $30.

At this time, something unique occurred in the history of industrial relations in Australia. For the first time, a case heard by Justice Moore was published in six different languages, the main languages that Ford workers spoke. Suddenly, even the Arbitration Commissioner realised that there was a language problem for the union as well as the employer and this changed the future of industrial relations not only at the Ford Motor Company and for Melbourne as a whole but also for the rest of Australia.

As a result of the strike and Justice Moore's decision, there was a very strong recommendation that Ford, as an employer, should improve its relationship with its employees, especially in regard to spoken communication. I believe Justice Moore also advised that the union should improve communication with its members as well.

Shortly after that, an ad appeared in the paper, advertising a job as liaison officer between management and employees. This person had to be familiar with languages and with various cultures and to act as a consultant. The paragraph caught my attention and I applied for the job, but the name of the company was not given.

It was the usual thing: I was interviewed by a management consultant and finally I was short-listed as one of six from amongst the dozen applicants who applied. I asked for the name of the company, but they refused to divulge it, which I took a very serious objection to. I finally found out the name and it turned out it was the Ford Motor Company and the job was as the 'Ethnic Consultant'. Somehow I must have gone down well because I was selected for the job and got the title of 'Employee Services Officer'. Basically I had to develop and maintain good relations amongst all the sections of the company.

In 1974, when Greece was fighting Turkey over Cyprus, I had in the soccer team two Cypriots – a Greek Cypriot and a Turkish Cypriot – and they were the best two players. When we won the cup, they were embracing each other and crying with joy and sharing a drink.

I was extremely happy to get that job. It was really what I wanted to do. It achieved an objective, a mission, I had of liaising between the various sections and of using my background, my management skills, my knowledge of language, my interests in culture, my desire to help. So it was with great satisfaction that I got the job and accepted it. And for all the frustrating times, it probably gave me the best sixteen years of my working life.

Of course, having accepted the job, although I had the best of intentions, I walked in at the worst possible time. The atmosphere was pretty bad when people came back to work after the strike, with a lot of the workers feeling they had been badly done by. Even the managers were not happy. A lot of them felt too many compromises had been made and there was no need for an ethnic affairs consultant, which was a reflection of their Anglo mindset. It was also a time when a lot of new workers were coming into the place — Turks for the first time, the Vietnamese started coming in — so there was a lot of inter-rivalry between those communities.

I remember one incident that started as a result of

a simple argument between a Lebanese worker and a Vietnamese worker and suddenly the word got out that it would carry on after hours. That afternoon, there were big lines of Lebanese cars coming from one door and Vietnamese from another, all armed with sticks and knives. The advice of management was to bring in the police, but I knew that both communities were wary and distrustful of the police and my advice was to have the police out of sight and to try to settle this with the interpreters, myself and the people. We sent a Vietnamese interpreter to head the Vietnamese section and explain to them that nothing will happen. I went into the Lebanese section telling the Lebanese to behave themselves. As it happened, thank God, the police didn't have to interfere.

Another day a very confronting situation arose with another two nationality groups because of a lack of trust. My idea was that we should do things to get people together rather than divide them. We had a social club that was pretty well dormant, so we started organising ethnic dances with various kinds of national music. To increase reading, we contacted the public library and asked them to service the area by coming into the canteen, which was a first in Australia. We formed a soccer club and a Credit Union — things that were going to meld the workforce together.

The soccer club was very successful because soccer is a powerful common denominator and the one thing that was uniting all migrant groups. Management gave us a ground, gave us money for uniforms and so on, and it took off. This really surprised the management, which had been trying to create football clubs without success. Its great success was in 1974, at the height of the Cyprus crisis, when Greece was fighting Turkey over Cyprus. In the team, I had two Cypriots — a Greek Cypriot and a Turkish Cypriot — and they were the best two players. When we won the cup, they were embracing each other and crying with joy and sharing a drink of lemonade. To me, that was the ultimate.

The library, the soccer club and the credit union, I felt, were successes in themselves. But they also helped create an atmosphere of trust between the various communities and show management that people could be trusted; that you could organise functions for people and that they would be appreciated; that friendship formed on the soccer field or in the canteen would reflect in the work situation. We didn't have a strike for quite a few years after that.

I also organised a nationality survey, I increased levels of interpreters, I added Vietnamese interpreters into our ranks, put Macedonian as well as Serb or Croat interpreters into the exercise. I created cultural awareness programs that were the very first in Australia for teaching people different cultural idiosyncrasies. It took years and years of constant effort and it changed migrant attitudes as much as it changed management attitudes.

I think it was also a unique era, when there were a lot of changes in the community at large. The Race Discrimination Act was being proclaimed, multiculturalism was being introduced and the White Australia Policy disappeared. There was a change from assimilation to integration. All of these happened just about simultaneously, acting as a catalyst to the general changes. And there was a bit of economic growth, which of course helped things. The big question was: When the cycle turns down, will it be sustainable or not?

Well, if I may summarise, I think Australians should be extremely proud of themselves, despite all the shortcomings, the factory fodder idea and the White Australia Policy. The activism of migrants in the 1950s and 60s was carried out in an evolutionary, rather than revolutionary, way and was supported by institutions that promoted multiculturalism, non-racism and equal opportunity in a concerned and responsible way. The Ford incident was an isolated, one-off case; so I think we should be very proud.

Australia became one of the few experiments in the world where multi-nationalism did occur, where race relationships were not harmed and where the ghetto situation did not occur. People quote Israel, but all of Israel has one thing in common: religion. Here, we even have multi-religious as well as multi-national factors. And hopefully, through the new generation, the future should be assured.

I am extremely pleased with the period during which I worked as an ethnic consultant, of the contribution I made. I feel I used my best assets, my ambitions, my idealism, my knowledge of language and my cultural background. I feel that those sixteen years, out of the forty I've been in Australia, were what I was brought up for.

Australia, to me, is a really wonderful country. It has given me happiness all the years that I have been here. That time has given me a material basis on which to practise my idealism without great loss. It has given me employment for all those years. But most important of all has been the human side: it has provided me with wonderful friendships, friendships with all nationalities.

Australia has also allowed me to set up my family, with three lovely young men who are all set and are good citizens of this country and who are proud Australians. They don't consider themselves as Anglo-Australians, but they do consider themselves to be worthwhile citizens, proud of their country and prepared to defend it if need be.

This country has allowed me to live a good life, out of the political troubles that are still going on in the Middle East — hate, race, and religious differences. And probably the best thing that Australia has given me has been peace of mind. You don't worry about your primary needs. You only worry about your secondary needs, which are not important. So I should be very, very thankful to Australia as a country. It has been wonderful and I hope it stays that way.

The activism of migrants was carried out in an evolutionary, rather than a revolutionary, way and was supported by institutions that promoted multiculturalism, non-racism and equal opportunity in a concerned and responsible way.

Our Tales

Will Davies and Andrea Dal Bosco

Will Since 1996, the postwar history of Australian migrants has been of continuing interest to both Andrea and me as film-makers. Yet each of us has had a very different migrant experience. It is an interesting fact that, while huge changes were taking place in the lives of migrants who came to Australia, for many native-born Australians, particularly in the 1950s, hardly an impact was felt from their arrival. Growing up as a kid in 1950s Australia, I was one of these; I had virtually no contact with 'new Australians' or the changes they brought to my homeland.

After the rationing and social dislocation of World War II, the 1950s dawned bright and optimistic for most Australians. My parents looked forward to a secure future in a country just starting to benefit from social prosperity and a booming economy. And for the ubiquitous middle class, life was the same. The returned servicemen and servicewomen collected in suburbs, assisted with land and low-cost housing loans.

Like so many others, my parents lived in a garage while their 'fibro' house was being built. The street was loose dirt with rain-scoured gutters — a great place to play. In those days the bread man came, as did the ice man and the milko. There was even the broom man; as a child, I always wondered how you made a living selling brooms door-to-door.

In this Anglo–urban environment, any migrant was a curiosity. Recollections are rare and fleeting, but I remember one boy in my infants' class in the mid-1950s who wore leather shorts and ate black bread sandwiches and smelled of what I now know as garlic. And a Czech family, the Stones. Mr Stone worked with my father in the airport suburb of Mascot and our families would meet at each other's homes. One strong recollection is a trip to Jenolan Caves where the Stones opened a thermos of coffee; this was the first time I had smelt coffee. Mr Stone also took wonderful pictures and even as a child I was drawn to this family, feeling they were very different and special, with a cultural style that excited me.

And this was the extent of my migrant experience — until my family moved to Leeton in the early 1960s and there I came across Italians for the first time. Suddenly a new cultural experience was opened up for me: new types of food, especially different fruit and vegetables; also the odd Italian delicacy, a cake that was different and real spaghetti. All for the first time.

I also met Italian kids for the first time and would go with them into their orchards and feast on fresh peaches. One kid had a field of watermelons and we'd take a ripe one and sit down on the canal bank and gorge ourselves, then go for a swim to clean up our messy bodies.

Another Italian boy showed me how to 'nick' peas at the Letona cannery. When the truck would come in loaded with peas still on the vines and would stop on the weighbridge, we'd sneak up and, clawing at the load, make off with armfuls of pea vines. We'd then sit across the road in the bush and eat raw peas until they went right through us, colour and all.

But this was the limit of my intersection with migrant people. It was only much later, at university, that I met others. I was always amazed at the personal sacrifice they had made in coming to Australia, leaving friends and family and starting a new life in an unknown and probably unfriendly place.

For Andrea, the experience was entirely different.

Andrea I approached the new millennium with two goals. The first was to make the second series of *Tales from a Suitcase* stronger than the first. And the second was to bottle my own pasta sauce at last.

Early in February I was already conducting research

On my first day at kindergarten I saw my first blonde-haired, blue-eyed, fair-skinned kid. I remember thinking God must have forgotten to colour him in.

interviews. I remember sitting in the living room of a beautiful old Croatian gentleman with blue eyes. He asked me, 'Why you want to make this show?'

With all my film-maker enthusiasm, I told him I wanted to make a series that paid tribute to the people who have changed the cultural face of Australia in the past fifty years and to show how far we have come as a multi-ethnic nation. His face suddenly lit up with the laughter of someone who has just heard the funniest joke of his life, while I sat there like a polite idiot trying to work out the punch line.

When he finally ran out of laughter he pinned me once again with his blue eyes and asked, 'How far you think we come?'

I said, 'A very, very long way. As a nation we finally accept and tolerate all cultures.' This time there was no laughter.

He said, 'Why I have to be tolerated? What am I — a bad smell, toilet paper? I don't want to be tolerated, I want to be appreciated.'

I am the first-born. My father arrived in Australia from Verona, Italy, on a two-year work contract in 1956. My mother arrived in 1964 from a tiny village called Rofrano in the province of Salerno, Italy. I was born in 1966 and brought up in an Italian house in Sydney's 'little Italy', Leichhardt. My first language was Italian. English was something that I learnt at school, the hard way.

> When I was a little boy, my parents felt the need to protect me from the Australians. On my first day at kindergarten I saw my first blonde-haired, blue-eyed, fair-skinned kid. I thought he had some kind of disease. I remember thinking God must have forgotten to colour him in. I honestly thought he was the strange one in my country where everyone spoke Italian and everyone looked like me, with dark hair, dark eyes and dark skin.

During my research I spoke to a woman who had just turned sixteen when World War II started. She was a Jewish girl living in Warsaw. In one afternoon in 1942 she lost her parents, her grandparents, her uncle and her brother. She was on her own. She decided to try and help others because she was fortunate enough to be born 'Aryan looking' — with fair skin and blonde hair — so she could credibly survive on Christian papers. She decided to hide six Jews in her home in Warsaw, imprisoning them in her walls in a bid to free them. After I listened to her story she asked me why I was so interested in her. I told her I thought that she was one of the most extraordinary women I'd ever met.

She replied, 'Anyone else in my situation would have done the same.'

> My fondest memories of growing up are of doing the 'woggie' things that have now become trendy, like bottling tomato sauce. I can still hear the 'clunk, clank, clunk, clank . . .' of my mother's tomato sauce machine as she hunched over it, turning the handle with one hand and feeding in the fresh tomatoes with the other. In the weeks leading up to the making of the sauce, we would start to scour the neighbourhood for beer bottles and scrutinise the fruit market for the best tomatoes at the best price. In my first participating year in this family ritual I started at the bottom of the ladder — as the

'basil stuffer'. My job was to push two leaves of basil into the bottles before my mother, hot on the trail of my young fingers, would ladle in the sauce.

The year 2000 was when I, together with my wife, was going to make the sauce. Making the sauce would be the easy part; convincing my wife of my Italo–Australian cultural need to do so would be the difficult ingredient in the recipe.

I remember, during my research, sitting with my domestic video-8 camera in the kitchen of a Greek woman who was telling me about the hunger and the misery that she experienced during World War II in her home country. She kept on looking at me in the eyes as she punctuated every story by saying, 'Do you know what is hunger, to be really hungry? To see people just lie down and die around you because there is nothing, nothing to eat? Do you know what hunger, real hunger, is? No, of course you don't. Why should you? I pray every day that this country always remains the "lucky" country.'

When I had finished talking to her and got up to leave, her daughter (who would have been old enough to be my mother) accompanied me to my car. She had been sitting out in the living room close to the kitchen, listening. I could see that she'd been crying, but I tried hard not to let on. She asked me for a copy of the research tape that I had just made of her mother talking. When I asked her why, she told me that she'd never heard what her mother had just told me. She finally understood why her mother would get furious if they ever left anything on their plates at teatime.

Every year, I discuss the tomato sauce with my wife, and every year she convinces me that I'm crazy for even entertaining such a thought.

'You can buy canned tomatoes, bottled tomatoes,

whatever-you-want tomatoes. Why go through this nightmare?'

So I never make the sauce . . .

That was until this year! The irony is that I was born and brought up in Australia; my wife was born and brought up in Italy. For me, being Australian means that I am free to make the sauce. For her, being Italian means that she can freely buy the sauce. The beauty of Australia for her is that most Italian products that she grew up with in Italy are only a shop away, while the beauty of Australia for me is that I can make the sauce the same way my mother made it.

I remember asking a Czech man what made him leave his country and he replied, 'I wanted to be free. I wanted to live in a country where I was not terrified of even thinking the wrong thing. Australia has no understanding of this. How can you know what a blue sky is if you have been blind all your life?'

Italo–Australian tradition demanded that I use recycled 750-millilitre beer bottles for the sauce: my first obstacle. Nearly all beer bottles these days are twist tops so it's impossible to re-cap them. But with a telephone call to my mother, I soon got over that hurdle and decided to use mineral water bottles. This was the first year that I was making the tomato sauce so I tapped into the old school of experience. I brought my mother to the fruit market to help me select my tomatoes. I always have to touch, squeeze, smell and taste the fruit to see if it's any good and even then I'm not sure, while my mother just has a quick glance and she knows.

What amazed me early on in my research was the humility of these old-timers. To sit and hear stories of great struggle and survival and then with the same breath the expression 'We survived.' Or: 'It could have been worse.' Or: 'It was nothing, really.'

I spoke to some sixty people from all parts of the world before we decided on the thirteen stories that would go to make up the second series of *Tales from a Suitcase*. Sixty amazing people with sixty amazing stories.

The moment that perhaps made me realise the importance of this series was when I was listening to an Italian man tell me of his life in the Queensland sugar cane fields. He described the pain of needing to *peel* his shirt off his body at night because the blood and sweat from the razor cuts inflicted by the cane leaves had dried it on.

His wife leaned over, when he went to the bathroom, and whispered in my ear, 'When he goes, that's it. Even the stones will cry.'

Even the stones will cry. That afternoon I realised that each one of these courageous old-timers is an Australian national treasure. They are the real pioneers who have paved the way in building the society that my generation enjoys today.

It's because of them that I'm free to make my sauce.

If this series and book achieve nothing else, I hope they achieve an awareness that the old person doddering in the shopping centre car park in the car ahead of you could be the same person who introduced gelato to Australia or helped build the Snowy Mountains Scheme. Australia's old are just as important as its young.

As for the sauce? Well the cream-coloured carpet in our apartment now has an interesting red pattern in certain places and of the forty bottles that we made, twelve didn't explode during the boiling process and it's only in the last few weeks that my wife has started talking to me again . . .